3000 QUOTATIONS

Sam Phillips

GOODWILL PUBLISHING HOUSE®
B-3 RATTAN JYOTI, 18 RAJENDRA PLACE
NEW DELHI -110008 (INDIA)

© Publishers

All rights reserved. No part of this publication may be reproduced; stored in a retrieval system or transmitted in any form or by any means, mechanical, photocopying or otherwise without the prior written permission of the publisher.

Published by
GOODWILL PUBLISHING HOUSE®
B-3 Rattan Jyoti, 18 Rajendra Place
New Delhi-110008 (INDIA)
Tel. : 25750801, 25820556
Fax : 91-11-25764396
E-mail : goodwillpub@vsnl.net
website : www.goodwillpublishinghouse.com

Printed at
B.B. Press, A-37, Sec-67, NOIDA-201301

A

ABILITY

The winds and waves are always on the side of the ablest navigators.
— *Edward Gibbon, Decline and Fall of Roman Empire*

There is great ability in knowing how to conceal one's ability.
— *Rochefoucauld*

Ability is poor man's wealth.
— *M. Wren*

To know how to hide one's ability is a great skill.
— *Rochefoucauld*

ABSENCE

Absence makes the heart grow fonder,
Isle of Beauty, Fare the well !
— *Thomas H. Bayly, Isle of Beauty*

Absence from those we love is self from self–a deadly banishment.
— *Shakespeare*

For there's nae luck about the house,
There's nae luck at a' :
There's little pleasure in the house.
When our gudeman's awa.'
— *William Julius Mickle, The Mariner's Wife*

Love reckons for months, and days for years and every little absence in an age.
— *Anon*

ABSENT-MINDEDNESS

My mind lets go a thousand things,
Like dates of wars and death of kings.
— *Thomas Baily Aldrich, Memory*

"The horror of that moment," the King went on, "I shall never, never forget !"

"You will, though," the Queen said, "If you don't make a memorandum of it."

— *Lewis Carroll*

Your absence of mind we have borne, till your presence of body came to be called in question by it.

— *Charles Lamb, Amecus Redivivus*

It is the disease of not listening, the malady of not marking, that I am troubled withal.

— *William Shakespeare, Ibid*

ABSTINENCE
Abstinence is as easy to me as temperance would be difficult.

ABUSE
Abuse is often of service.

— *Johnson*

Abuse me as often as you will; it is often a benefit than any injury.

— *E. Nott*

ACCENT
Accent is the soul of language; it gives to it both feeling and truth.

— *Rousseao*

ACCIDENTS
Accidents will occur in the best regulated families and in families not regulated by that persuading influence which sanctifies while it enhance — I would say, in short, by the influence of Woman in the lofty character of Wife.

— *Dickens, David Copperfield*

Accident counts for much in companionship as in Marriage.

— *Henry Brooks Adams, The Education Henry Adams*

ACCURACY
Accuracy is the twin brother of honesty, inaccuracy of dishonesty.

— *C. Simmons*

ACHIEVEMENT
Death comes to all
But great achievements raise a monument
Which shall endure until the sun grows cold.
— *Georgius Fabricus*

ACTING AND ACTOR
Have patience with the jealousies and petulances of actors, for their hour is their eternity.
— *Richard Garnett, Ibid Preface*

As in a theatre, the eyes of men,
After a well graced actor leaves the stage,
Are idly bent on him that enters next,
Thinking his rattle to be tedious.
— *William Shakespeare, Ibid*

On the stage he was natural, simple, affecting :
'Twas only that when he was off he was acting.
— *Oliver Goldsmith, Retaliation*

ACQUAINTANCE
Sudden acquaintance brings repentance.
— *Thomas Fuller*

If a man is worth knowing at all, he is worth knowing well.
— *Alexander Smith*

ACQUIREMENT
Every noble acquisition is attended with risks; he who fears to encounter the one, must not expect to obtain the other.
— *Metastasio*

ACTION
Think in the morning, act in the noon, eat in the evening, sleep in the night.
— *William Blake*

The actions of men are the best interpreters of their thoughts.
— *Locke*

The actions of men are like the index to a book; they point out what is most remarkable in them.
— *Thomas*

The great end of life is not knowledge but action.
— *Thomas Henry Huxley*

I wish to preach, not the doctrine of ignoble ease but the doctrine of the strenuous life.
— *Theodore Roosevelt, Speech before the Amiltion Club, Chicago (April 10, 1899)*

Actions are our; their consequences belong to heaven.
— *Sir P. Francis*

Strong reasons make strong actions.
— *Shakespeare, King John*

ADAM AND EVE
Whilst Adam slept, Eve from his side arose :
Strange his first sleep should be his last repose.
— *Anon, The Consequences*

In Adam's fall
We sinned all.
— *New England Primer*

Oh, Adam was a gardener, and God made him seed.
That half a proper gardener's work is done upon his knees.
— *Rudyard Kipling, Ibid*

She gave me of the tree, and I did eat.
— *John Milton*

So curses all Eve's daughters of what complexion soever.
— *William Shakespeare, Ibid*

There is no ancient gentleman but gardeners ...... they hold up Adam's profession.

ADDRESS
Brahma once asked of force, 'Who is stronger than thou'? She replied, "Address".
— *Victor Hugo*

ADMIRATION
Yet let not each gay turn the rapture move;
For fools admire, but men of sense approve.
— *Alexander Pope*

Admistration is very short-lived passion that immediately decays upon growing familiar with its object.
— Addison, The Spectator

ADULTERY
She named the infant "Pearl" at being of great price purchased with all she had.
— Nathaniel Hawthorne, Ibid

What men call gallantry, and gods adultery.
Is much more common where the climate's sultry.
— Byron, Don Juan, I

It is a wise father that knows his own child.
— William Shakespeare

ADVANTAGE
The ass will carry his load, but not a double load :
ride not a free horse to death
— Miguel De Cervantes

Advantage is a better soldier than rashness.
— Shakespeare, Henry V

For when I gave you an inch, you took an ell
— Johan Heywood, Ibid

ADVENTURE
Adventure was his coronal.
And all his wealth was wandering
— Henry Hervert Knibbs

The day shall not be up so soon as I.
To try the fair adventure of tomorrow.
— William Shakespeare, Ibid

ADVERSITY
Sweet are the uses of adversity.
Which, like the toad, ugly and venomous.
Wears yet a precious jewel in his head.
— William Shakespeare, As you Like it

Prosperity is not without many fears and distastes; and adversity is not without comforts and hopes.
— Francis Bacon

Adversity introduces a man to himself.
— *Avon*

Affliction may one day smile again; and till then, sit thee down, sorrow !
— *William Shakespeare*

Prosperity is no just scale; adversity is the only balance to weigh friends.
— *Proverb*

ADVERTISEMENT

You can tell the ideals of a nation by its advertisements.
— *Douglas, South Wind*

Sanely applied advertising could remake the world.
— *Stuart Chase*

Good wine needs neither bush nor preface.
To make it welcome.
— *Sir Walter Scott, Peveril of the Peak*

ADVICE

Never trust the advice of a man in difficulties
— *Aesop, The Fox and the Goat*

When a man seeks your advice, he generally wants your praise.
— *Chesterfield*

And with my advice, faith you'd take me.
— *Samual Lover, Window Machree*

Ask a woman advice, and
Whatever she advise.
Do the very reverse and you're
Sure to be wise.
— *Thomas Moore, Make a Good Politician*

To accept good advice is but to increase one's ability
— *Goethe*

We give advice by the bucket, but take it by the grain.
— *W.R. Alger*

Advice is seldom welcome, those who need it most like it least.
— *Johnson*

AFFECTATION
We have been, let us say, to hear the latest Pole.
Transmit the preludes, through his hair and fingertips.
— *Thomas Stearns Eliot, Portrait of a Lady*

Affection is a greater enemy to the face than the smallpox.
— *St. Evermond*

AFFLICTION
Ah ! If you only knew the peace, there is in an accepted sorrow.
— *Madame Guion*

The Lord gets his best soldiers out of the high-land of affliction.
—*Spurgeon*

AGE
I have lived long enough; my way of life,
Is fall's into sear, the yellow leaf.
— *Shakespeare, Macbeth*

No wise man ever wished to be younger.
— *Swift*

Grabbed age and youth cannot live together.
— *Shakespeare, The Passionate Pilgrim*

Old wood best to burn, old wine to drink, old friends to trust and old authors to read.
— *Bacon*

AGITATION
Agitation is the marshalling of the conscience to a nation to mould its laws.
— *Sir Robert Peel*

AGREEMENT & AGREEABILITY
I do not want people to be very agreeable, as it saves me the trouble of linking them a great deal.
— *Jane Austen*

He that complies against his will,
Is of his own opinion still.
— *Samuel Butler*

We hardly find any person of good sense save those who agree with us.
— *Rochefoucauld*

Agreed to differ.
> — *Robert Southey, Life of Wesley*

AIR

And seem to walk on wings and trend in air.
> — *Alexander Pope*

Holla your name to the reverberate hills,
And make the babbling gossip of the air.
Cry out.
> — *William Shakespeare*

Where they (birds) most breed and haunt, I have observed.
The air is delicate.
> — *William Shakespeare*

ALE

Dost thou think, because thou are virtuous, there shall be no more cakes and ale ?
> — *William Shakespeare, Twelfth Night*

Back and side go bare, go bare;
Both foot and hand go cold;
But belly, God send thee good ale enough,
Whether it be new or old.
> — *John Still, Grammer Gurto i's Needle*

Then to the spicy nut-brown ale.
> — *John Milton*

I would give all my fame for a pot of ale and safety.
> — *William Shakespeare*

All-powerful Ale ! whose sorrow-seething sweets.
Oft I repeat in vacant afternoon.
> — *Thomas Warton*

ALLAH

Praise be to Allah, the Lord of creation,
The merciful, the Compassionate.
Ruler of the Day of Judgement
Help us, lead us in the path.
> — *Mohamed, Koran.*

ALLEGORIES

Allegories are fine ornaments and good illustrations, but no proof.
> — *Luther*

ALLIANCES
Peace, commerce and honest friendship with all nations entangling alliance with one.
— *Jefferson, First Inaugural Address*

ALLEY
Of all the girls that are so smart,
There's none like pretty Sally,
She is the darling of my heart,
And she lives in our alley.
— *Hanry Carey*

ALLITERATION
Begot by butchers, by beggars bred.
Howe high his Honour hold his haughty head.
— *Anon*

ALTRUISM
He never errs who sacrifices self.
— *Lord Lytton : New Timon*

AMBASSADOR
An ambassador is an honest man sent to lie and intrigue abroad for the benefit of his country.
— *Sir H. Wotton*

AMBITION
Cromwell, I charge thee, fling away ambition;
By that sin fell the angels.
— *Shakespeare : Henry VIII*

Valuting ambition which overleaps itself.
—*Shakespeare*

Desire of greatness is a godlike sin.
— *Dryden : Absalom and Achitophel*

AMIABILITY
How easy to be amiable in the midst of happiness and success.
— *Madame Swetchine*

AMUSEMENT
Amusement to an observing mind in study.
— *Disraeli*

ANARCHY
Anarchy is hatred of human authority, atheism of divine authority—two sides of the same whole.
— *Macphetron*

ANCESTRY
The man who has not anything to bost of but his illustrious ancestors is like a potato—the only good belonging to him is underground.
— *Sir Thomas Overbury, Characters*

Breed is stronger than pasture.
— *George Eliot*

Birth is nothing where virtue is not.
— *Moliere*

ANGEL
Look homeward, Angel, now, and melt with truth.
— *Milton Lycidas*

And flights of angels sing thee to the rest.
— *Shakespeare, Hamlet*

We are like angels till our passion dies.
— *Decker*

ANGER
Anger is short madness.
— *Horace Epistles*

To be angry is revenge the faults of others on ourselves.
— *Pope*

Anger makes dull men witty, but it keeps them poor.
— *Bacon*

Anger is one of the sinews of soul.
— *Fuller*

To be furious
Is to be frightened out of fear, and in that mood, the dove will peck the estridge.
— *Shakespeare, Antony and Cleopatra*

ANTICIPATION
He who foresees calamities suffers them twice over.
— *Porteous*

Nothing is good as it seems beforehand
— *George Eliot*

ANTIQUITY
Those we call the ancients were really new in everything.
— *Pascal*

ANXIETY
It's a melancholy consideration indeed that our chief comforts often produce our greatest anxieties, and that an increase of our passions is but an inlet to new disquietudes.
— *Goldsmith, The Good Natured Man*

Do not anticipate trouble, of worry about what may never happen. Keep in the sunlight.
— *Franklin*

APOLOGY
Apology is only egotism wrong side out.
— *Holmes*

Apologies only account for the evil which they cannot alter.
— *Disraeli*

APPAREL
Costly the habit as the purse can buy,
But not expressed in fancy; rich not gaudy;
For the apparel oft proclaims the man.
— *Swift, Hamlet*

APPEARANCE
She looks as if butter wouldn't melt in her mouth
— *Swift, Polite Conversation*

All that glitters is not gold;
Gilded tombs do worms unfold.
— *Shakespeare, Merchant of Venice*

Foolish men mistake transitory semblances for eternal fact, and go astray more and more.
— *Carlyle*

APPETITE
Now good digestion wait on appetite, and health on both.
— *Shakespeare*

APPLAUSE
In the vain laughter of folly wisdom bears half applause.
— *George Eliot, Romola*

APRIL
Oh, to be in England
Now that April's there.
— *R. Browning, Home Thought Abroad*

ARCHITECTURE
A Gothic church is petrified religion.
—*Coleridge*

ARGUMENT
He draweth out the thread of his verbosity finer than the staple of his argument.
— *Shakespeare, Love's Labour Lost.*

Clear statement is argument.
— *W.G.T. Shedd*

Wise men argue cause : fools decide them.
— *Anacharsis*

ARMY
The best armour is to keep out of gunshot.
— *Bacon*

Army is a good book in which to study human life.
— *De Vigny*

ARROGANCE
Nothing is more hateful to a poor man than the purseproud arrogance of rich.
— *Cumberland*

ART
Art is long and time is fleeting
— *Longfellow, A Psalm of Life*

A life of sacrifice is the pinnacle of art and is full of true joy.
— *Mahatma Gandhi*

Art lies in concealing art.
— *Ovid, Art of Love*

Art hath in enemy called ignorance.
— *Bern Johnson*

All art is but imitation of nature.
— *Seneca, Epistle of Lucllius*

ASKING
I am prejudiced in favour of him who, without imprudence, can ask boldly.
— *Lavater*

ASPIRATION
Long is the way
And hard, that out of hell leads up to light.
— *John Milton, Paradise Lost*

They build too low who build beneath the skies.
— *Young, Night Thoughts*

Man can climb to the highest summits but he cannot dwell there long.
— *G.B. Shaw*

ASSERTION
Assertion, unsupported by fact, is nugatory.
— *Junius*

ASSOCIATE
Tell me with whom thou art found, and I will tell thee who thou art.
— *Goethe*

ASSOCIATED
There is no man who hath not some interesting association.
— *Alison*

ASTRONOMY
No undevout astronomer is mad.
— *Young, Essays on Atheism*

ATHEISM
Atheism is rather in the lip than in the heart of man.
— *Bacon, Essays on Atheism*

By night an atheist shall believe in God.
— *Young*

The fool hath said in his heart, there is no God.
— *Old Testament, Psalms*

ATTENTION
Attention makes the genius : all learning, fancy sincere, and skill depend upon it.
— *Wilmott*

AUTHORITY
Authority forgets a dying king.
— *Tennyson, The Passing Arthur*

Though authority be stubborn bear, yet he is oft led by the nose with gold.
— *Shakespeare, Winte's Tail*

The highest duty is to respect authority.
— *Pope Leo XII*

AUTHORSHIP
No man but a blockhead ever wrote except for money.
— *Johnson, Remark*

The chief glory of every people arise from its authors.
— *Johnson*

The author himself is the best judge for his performance.
— *Gibbon, Memories of My Life and Writings*

AUTUMN
When chill November's surely blast.
Made fields and forests bare.
— *Robert Burns, Man was made to Mourn*

Season of mist and mellow fruitlessness.
—*Keats*

AVARICE
Avarice, the spur of industry.
— *Thomas Hughes, Essays of Civil Liberty*

Avarice is the vice of declining years.
— *Bancroft*

AVIATION
In aeronautics one finds new things only by looking for them.
— *Clerve*

B

BABIES
Babies do not want to hear about babies, they like to be told of giants and castles, and that which can stretch and stimulate their little minds.
— *Samuel Johnson, Miscellanies*

A rose with all its sweetest leaves yet unfolded
— *Byron*

BACHELORS
No the world must be peopled. When I said I would die a bachelor, I did not think I should live till I were married.
— *Shakespeare, Much Ado About Nothing*

All reformers are bachelors.
— *George More, The Bending of the Bough*

Because I will not do the wrong to mistrust any, I will do myself the right to trust none; I will live a bachelor.
— *Shakespeare*

BALLAND
Ballands are vocal portraits of the national mind.
— *Lamb*

BANK
The Banker is a man who lends you an umbrella when the weather is fair and takes it away when it rains.
— *Anon*

BASENESS
Every base occupation makes one sharp in its practice, and dull in every other.
— *Sir P. Sidney*

BEARD
Beard was never the true standard of brains.
— *Fuller*

BEAUTY
There is no excellent beauty that hath and not some strangeness in the proportion.
— *Francis Bacon, Essays of Beauty*

The best part of beauty is that which no picture can express.
— *Bacon*

A thing of beauty is a joy for ever;
Its loveliness increases : it will never
Pass into nothingness.
Beauty is truth's smile.
— *Keats*

When she beholds her own face in a perfect mirror.
— *Tagore, Fireflies*

Ay; beauty's princely majesty is such,
Confounds the tongue and makes the senses rough.
— *Shakespeare, Henry VI*

Beauty is a short-lived reign.
— *Socrates*

BED
Early to bed early to rise.
Makes a man healthy, wealthy and wise.
— *Franklin, Poor Richard's Almanac for 1735*

To rise with the lark, and go to bed with the lamb.
— *Nicholas Breton, Court of Country*

O bed, delicious bed !
That heaven upon earth to the weary head.
— *Hood, Miss Kismansegg*

BEGGAR
Beggars must not be choosers.
— *Beaumont and Fletchers, Scornful Lady*

Borrowing is not much better than begging.
— *Lessing, Nathan the wise*

He who begs timidly courts refusal.
— *Seneca, Hippalytue*

Better a living beggar than a buried emperor.
— *Burton, Anatomy of Melancholy*

BEHAVIOUR

Do wrong to none.
— *Shakespeare, All's Well that Ends Well*

Those that are good mannered at the court are as ridiculous in the country as the behaviour of the country is most mockable at the court.
— *Shakespeare, As You Like It*

BELIEF

Blessed are they that have not seen, and yet have believed.
— *New Testament, John XX, 29*

A man must not swallow more belief than he can digest.
— *Haxelock Hills, The Dance of Life*

A thing that nobody belives cannot be proved too often.
— *G.B. Shaw, Devil's Disciple*

BELLS

Ring out the old, ring in the new,
Ring, Happy bells across the snow.
— *Tennyson, In Memoriam*

Who is to bell the cat. It is easy to propose impossible remedies.
— *Acheson*

BENEFIT

To do well to bad man is as great a danger as to do in a good one.
— *Ploutus, Panulus*

BENEVOLENCE

He child their wanderings but relieved their pain.
— *Goldsmith, Deserted Village*

Benevolent feeling ennobles the most trifling actions.

BEREAVEMENT

What, all my pretty chickens and their dam.
At one fell swoop ?
— *Shakespeare, Macbeth*

BIBLE
Alone at night,
I read my Bible more any Euclid less.
— *Robert Buchanan*

The book of books, the storehouse and magazine of life and comfort, the Holy Scriptures.
— *Herbert, Priest to the Temple*

The Bible is a window in this prison of hope through which we may look into eternity.
— *Dwight*

BIOGRAPHY
Would that every Johnson in the world had his vertical Boswell or leash of Boswells.
— *Carlyle, Voltaire*

Biography is the most universally pleasant and profitable of all reading.
— *Carlyle*

BIRTH
The pleasing punishment that women bear.
— *Shakespeare, Comedy, of Errors*

What it is that we rejoice at a birth and grieve at a funeral? It is because we are not the person concerned?
— *Mark Twain, Pudd'nhead Wilson's Calendar*

Lady you are the cruellest alive.
If you will lead those graces to the grave.
And leave the world no copy.
— *Shakespeare, Twelfth Night*

BIRTHPLACE
Every man has a lurking wish to appear considerable in his native place.
— *Johnson, Letter 1770*

BITTERNESS
But hushed be every thought that springs.
From out the bitterness of things.
— *Wordsworth, Elegiac*

BLESSING
I had most need of blessing and "Amen"
Struck in my throat
— *Shakespeare, Macbeth*

"God bless us every one!" said Tiny Tim, the last of all :
— *Dickens, A Christmas Carol*

BLINDNESS
They be blind leaders of the blind. And if the blind lead the blind, both shall fall into the ditch.
— *New Testament, Mathew*

To live a life half dead a living death.
— *Milton, Samson Agonistes*

BLISS
It was a dream of perfect bliss
Too beautiful to last
— *T.K. Bayly, It was a Dream*

BLOCKHEAD
A blockhead cannot come in, nor go away, nor sit, nor rise, nor stand, like a man of sense.
— *Bruyere*

BLOOD
Blood is thicker than water
— *John Ray, English Prov.*

Feat at my heart, as at a cup. My life-blood seem'd to sip.
— *Samuel Taylor Coleridge*

BLUNDERS
It was worse than a crime; it was blunder.
— *Fouche*

It is disgraceful to stumble twice against the same stone.
— *Greek Proverb*

BLUNTNESS
The rudeness is a sense to his good wit
Which gives men stomach to digest his words with better appetite.
— *Shakespeare, Julius Caeser*

BLUSH
Better a blush on the face than blot on the heart.
— *Cervante*

A blush is the colour of virtue
— *Diogenes*

BLUSTERING
A killing tongue, but a quiet sword.
— *Shakespeare*

BOASTING
Ah, this thou should'nt have done,
And not have spoke on't;
— *Shakespeare, Antony and Cleopatra*

Where boasting ends, there dignity begins.
— *Young*

BODY
A healthy body is a guest chamber for the soul; a sick body is a prison.
— *Bacon*

If anything is sacred the human body is sacred.
— *Walt Whitman, I Sing the Body Electric*

BOLDNESS
What action is to the orator, that boldness is to the public man first, second and third.
— *Bacon, Insurative*

I dare do all that may become a man;
Who dare do more is none.
— *Shakespeare, Macbeth*

Fools rush in where angels fear to tread.
— *Pope*

BOOKS
Books without the knowledge of life are useless, for what should books teach but the art of living ?
— *Johnson*

Laws die, Books never.
— *Bulwer, Lytton*

A good book is the precious life-blood of a master spirit, embalmed and treasured up on purpose to a life beyond life.
— *Milton, Areopagitica*

Dreams, books, are each a world, and books, we know.
— *Wordsworth, Personal Talk*

Some books are to be tasted, others to be swallowed and some few to be chewed and digested.
— *Bacon, Essays of Studies*

Books are the shrine where the saint is, or is believed to be.
— *Bacon, To Sir Bodely*

BOOTS
'Boots......boots......boots......boots movin' up and down again. There's no discharge in the war!
— *Kipling, Boots*

BORE
The secret of boring is the practice of saying everything.
— *Voltaire*

One of the best things in the world to be is a bore; it requires no experience, but needs some practice to be a good one.
— *Charles Dudley Warner, Being a Boy*

BORROWING
The borrower is servant to the lender.
— *Proverb*

Neither a borrower nor a lender be
For loan oft loses both itself and friend,
And borrowing dulls the edge of husbandry.
— *Shakespeare*

BOY
The smiles and tears of boyhood's years.
The words of love then spoken.
— *Thomas Moore, Oft in the Silly Night*

BRAVE
The best hearts are ever the bravest.
— *Sterne*

BREAD
Man shall not live by bread alone.
— *Mathew, Old Testament*

O, God! that bread should be so dear,
And flesh and blood so cheap!
— *Thomas Hood, The Song of the Shirt*

BREEDING
Good breeding is the blossom of good sense.
— *Young, Love of Fame*

BREVITY
Brevity is the soul of wit.
— *Shakespeare, Hamlet*

Since brevity is the soul of wit,
And tediousness the limits and outward flourishers I will be brief.
— *Shakespeare, Hamlet*

BRIBERY
Every man has his price.
— *Sir Robert Walpole*

Judges and senates have been bought for gold.
Esteem and love were never to be sold.
— *Pope, Essay on Man*

Too poor for a bribe, and too pround to importune. He had not the method of making a fortune.
— *Gray, On his Own Character*

BROTHER
Am I brother's keeper ?
— *Old Testment, Genesis, IV*

A brother is a friend given by nature.
— *J.B. Legouv*

BROTHERHOOD
No distance breaks the tie of blood;
Brothers are brothers evermore.
Father and mother
Ask reverence; a brother only love.
— *Tennyson, In Memoriam*

There is no brotherhood of man without the fatherhood of God.
— H.M. Field

BRUTALITY
The conviction of the justification of using even most brutal weapons is always dependent on the presence of a fanatical belief in the necessity of the victory of a revolutionary new order on this globe.
— Adolf Hitler, Mein Kampf.

BUILD
He built it better than he knew;
The conscious stone to beauty grew.
— Emerson, The Problem

BULLFIGHT
It is impossible to believe the emotional and spiritual intensity and pure, classic beauty that can be produced by a man, an animal, and piece of scarlet serge draped over a sick.
— Earnest Hemingway, Death in the Afternoon

BUSINESS
That which is everybody's business is nobody's business.
— Izaak Walton, The Complete Angler

Business to-day consists in persuading crowds.
— Gerald Stanley Lee, Crowds

The man who is above the business may one day find his business above him.

BUT
The meanest, most contemptible kind of praise is that which first speaks well of a man, and then qualified with a 'but'.
— H.W. Beecher

CAESAR
Imperious Caesar, dead and turn'd to clay,
Might stop a hole to keep the wind away.
— *Shakespeare, Hamlet V*

CALAMITY
He who foresees calamities suffers them twice over.
— *Porteus*

Love frees all toils but one,
Calamity and it can ill agree.
— *Beaumont and Fletcher, The Laws of Candy*

CALM
Calm appears when storms are past;
Love will have its hour at last.
— *Dryden, The Secular Mask*

CALUMNY
Be thou as chaste as ice, as pur as snow, thou shall not escape calumny.

Calumny will sear Virtue itself.
— *Shakespeare, Winter's Tale*

Cutting honest throats by whisper.
— *Scott*

CALVINISM
Calvinism is a democratic and republican religion.
— *Be Tocqueville*

CANDLE
Neither do men light a candle, and put it under a bushel but on a candlestick, an it giveth light unto all that are in the house.
— *New Testament, Mathew V*

CANDOUR
Unto the end shall charity endure.
And candour hide those faults it cannot cure.
— *Churchil, The Apology*

I want that glib and oil art,
To speak and purpose not.
— *Shakespeare*

CANT
My dear friend, clear your mind of cant.
— *Johnson, Remark to Boswell*

You may talk as other people do; you may say to a man, Sir, I am your most humble servant. You are not his most humble servant.
— *Johnson, Letter to Lord Chesterfield*

CAPITALISM
Capitalism production begets, with the inexorability of law of nature, its own negation.
— *Carl Marx, Capital*

CAPTIVITY
The desert is imprisoned in the wall of its unbounded barrenness.
— *Tagore, Fireflies*

CARD
Every pack of cards is malicious libel on courts and on the world.
— *Southey*

See how the world its veteran reward;
A youth of frolics, an old age of cards.
— *Pope, Moral Essays*

CARE
Care is not cure, but rather corrosive,
For things that are not to be remedied.
— *Henry VI*

To carry care to bed, is to sleep with a pack on your back.
— *Haliburton*

CARICATURE
Take my advice, and draw caricature. By the long practice of its have lost the enjoyment of beauty.
— *Hagrath*

CARELESSNESS
For want of timely care
Millions have died of medicable wounds.
— *Armstrong, Art of Preserving Health*

CASTLES
If you built castles in the air, your work need not be lost, there is where they should be. Not put foundation under them.
— *Thoreau*

CAUSE
Everything in nature is a cause from which there flows some effect.
— *Spinoza*

Great causes are never tried on their merits.
— *Emerson, Essays*

God befriend us, as our cause, is just!
— *Shakespeare, Henry*

Self can mould the brightest cause or gild the worst.
— *T. Moore, The Sceptic*

CAUTION
Look before you leap; see before you go.
— *Tusser*

A wise man does not trust all his eggs to one basket.
— *Cervantes*

Early and provident ear is the mother of safety.
— *Burke, Speech, 1972*

CAVALIER
Marching along fifty score strong.
And if don't hurt her, she'll do me no harm.
— *Jane Taylor, I Like Little Pussy*

CENSURE
Thou best humoured man with the words humoured muse.
— *Goldsmith, Retaliation*

Forbear to judge, for we are sinners all.
— *Shakespeare*

Censure is the tax a man pays to the public for being eminent.
— Swift, Thoughts on various subjects

CEREMONY
Ceremony is the invention of wise men to keep fools at a distance.
— Steele

A table full of welcome makes scarce one dainty dish.
— Shakespeare, Comedy of Errors

CHANCE
Chance is perhaps the pseudonym of God when he did not want to sign.
— Anatole France, The Garden of Epicurus

Under the bludgeonings of chance.
My head is bloody, but unbowed.
— W.E. Heleny, Invictus

CHANGE
It is not strange that even our loves should change with our fortune.
— Shakespeare

Things do not change, we change.
— Thoreau, Walden

Change is the strongest son of life.
— George Meredith, Woops of Waterman

CHARACTER
Character is what you are in the dark.
— Dwight L. Moody, Sermons

Character must be kept bright as well as clean.
— Dora Chesterfield, Letter to His Son

The great hope of society is individual Character.
— Ganning

CHARITY
Charity gives itself rich; covetousness hoards itself poor.
— German Proverb

The charities that soothe, and heal, and bless, lie scattered at the feet of men lie flowers.
— Wordsworth

The place of charity, like that of God, is everywhere.

— *Quarles*

CHARM
Charms strike the sight
But merit wins the soul.

— *Pope, The Rape of the Lock*

CHASTITY
My chastity of honour, which feels a stain like a wound.

— *George Eliot*

That chastity's the jewel of our house.

— *Shakespeare, All's Well That Ends Well*

CHEATING
Don't steal; thou'lt never thus compete.
Successfully in business, Cheat.

— *Ambrose Pierce, The Devil's Dictionary*

CHEERFULNESS
A light heart lives long.

— *Shakespeare*

I had rather have a fool to make me merry, than experience to make me sad.

— *Shakespeare*

CHILD
In the child the father's image lies.

— *Shakespeare, Rape of the Lucre*

The child is the father of man.

— *Wordsworth, My Heart Leaps Up*

CHILDHOOD
The childhood shows the man, as morning shows the day.

— *Milton*

CHILDREN
Children have more need of models than of critics.

— *Joubert*

From the solemn gloom of the temple children run out to sit in the dust, God watches them play and forgets the priest.

— *Tagore*

CHIVALRY
The age of chivalry is never past, so long as there is a wrong left unredressed on earth.
— *Charles Kingsley*

But the age of chivalry is gone; that of sophisters, economists, and calculators has succeeded.
— *Edmund Burke, Reflections on the French Revolution*

CHOICE
God offers to every mind its choice between truth and repose.
— *Emerson, Essays; Intellect*

There's small choice in rotten apples.
— *Shakespeare, Taming of the Shrew*

Of two evils we take the less.
— *Richard Hooker, Lake of Ecclesiastical Polity*

CHRIST
All history is incomprehensible without Christ.
— *Earnest Renan, Life of Jesus*

I believe Plato and Socrates. I believe in Jesus Christ.
— *Coleridge*

Must then Christ perish in torment in every age to save hose that have no imagination ?
— *Bernard Shaw, Saint John*

CHRISTIAN
A Christian is Good Almighty's gentleman.
— *J.C. & A.W. Hare*

A Christian is the highest style of man.
— *Young*

CHRISTIANITY
Christianity taught men that love is worth more than intelligence.
— *Jacquer Marition, I Believe*

CIRCUMSTANCES
Circumstances are more powerful than man.
— *Nehru*

Circumstances! I make circumstances.
— *Napoleon*

Men are the sport of circumstances, when the circumstances seem the sport of men.
— *Byron*

CIRCUS
Bread and circus games
— *Juvenal, Satires*

CITY
Fields and trees teach me nothing, but the people in a city do.
— *Socrates, Plato*

The people are the city.
— *Shakespeare*

God the first garden made, and Cain the first City.
— *Cowley*

CIVILITY
Nothing costs less, nor is cheaper, than the compliments of good women.
— *Cervante*

CIVILIZATION
Comfort, opportunity, number, and size are not synonymous with civilization
— *Abraham Flexner, Universities*

Nations like individuals, live and die; but civilization survives.
— *Mazzin*

A sufficient measure of civilization is the influence of good women.
— *Emerson*

The ultimate tendency of civilization is towards barbarism.
— *Hare*

CLEANLINESS
Certainly this is a duty, not a sin.
"Cleanliness is indeed next to godliness."
— *John Wesley, Sermon XCII on Dress*

Beauty commonly produces love, but cleanliness preserves it.
— *Addison*

Beauty will fade and perish, but personal cleanliness is practically undying, for it can be renewed whenever it discovers symptoms of decay.
— *W.S. Gilbert, The Sorcerer*

God loveth the clean.
— *The Koran*

CLEARNESS
And if the mind will clear conceptions glow,
The willing words in just expression flow.
— *P. Frencies Horace, Art of Poetry*

CLEMENCY
As meekness moderates anger, so clemency moderates punishment.
— *Stretch*

CLEVER
Clever men are good, but they are not the best.
— *Carlyle*

Be good, sweet maid, and let who can be clever.
— *Charles Kingsley, A Farewell*

CLOTHING
The clothes make the man.
— *Latin Proverb*

They just wore
Enough for modesty no more
— *A Buchanam, White Rose and Red*

CLOUD
Clouds are hill in vapour, hills are clouds in stone — a phantasy is time's dream.
— *Tagore, Fireflies*

Those playful fancies of the mighty sky.
— *Albert Smith*

COERCION
The more the fire is covered up the more it burns.
— *Ovid, Metam*

COLOURS
The purest and most thoughtful minds are those which love colour the most.
— *Ruskin, Stones of Venice*

Colours speak all languages.
— *Addison, The Spectator*

Light finds her treasure of colours through the antagonism of clouds.
— *Tagore, Fireflies*

COMBAT
So frowned the mighty combatants, that hell grew darker at their frown.
— *Milton, Paradise Lost*

COMFORT
A house full of books, and a garden of flowers.
— *A. Lang, Bellads of True Wisdom*

Most of our comforts grow up between our crosses.

COMMANDER
It is better to have a lion at the head of an army of sheep, than a sheep at the head of an army of lions.
— *De Foe*

COMMERCE
A true bred merchant is the best gentleman of the nation.
— *De Foe, Robinson Crusoe*

Commerce is the equalizer of the wealth of nations.
— *Gladstone*

COMMON SENSE
Common sense is in spite of, not the result of education.
— *Victor Hugo*

Common sense is not so common.
— *Voltaire*

Common sense is, of all kinds, the most uncommon.
— *Toron Edward*

COMPANIONS

Associate yourself with men of good quality if you esteem your own reputation; for its better to be alone than in a bad company.
— *George Washington, Rules of Civility*

Good company and good discourse are the very sinews of virtue.
— *Izaak Walton*

COMPARISON

Hyperion to a satyr, Thersites to Hercules, mud to marble, dunghil to diamond, a singed cat to a Bengale tiger, a whinning pupy to a roaring lion.
— *James G. Blaine*

The superiority of some men is merely local—They are great because their associates are little.
— *Johnson*

COMPASSION

Teach me to feel another's woe,
To hide the fault I see :
That mercy I do others show,
That mercy show to me.
— *Pope, Universal Prayer*

The dew of compassion is a tear.
— *Byron*

COMPETENCE

A competence is vital to content;
Much wealth is corpulence, if not disease.
— *Young, Night Thoughts*

COMPLAINING

The wheel that squeaks the loudest
Is the one that gets the grease.
— *Josh Billings, The Kicker*

Those who do not complain are never pitied.
— *Jane Austen*

Complaint is the largest tribute Heaven receives.
— *Swift*

I am a love-lorn creature …… and everything goes contrary with me.
— *Dickens, David Copperfield*

COMPLIMENTS
Compliments are only lies in courtclothes.
— *Anon*

COMPROMISE
Life cannot subsist in society but by reciprocal concessions.
— *Johnson*

All great alteration in human affairs are produced by compromise.
— *Sydney Smith*

CONCEALMENT
It is great cleverness to know how to conceal our cleverness.
— *Rochefoucauld*

CONCEIT
Conceit in weakest bodies strongest works.
— *Shakespeare, Hamlet*

He was like the cock who thought the sun had risen to hear him crow.
— *George Eliot, Adam Beep*

Wind puffs up empty bladders; opinion, fools.
— *Socrates*

CONDUCT
The integrity of men is to be measured by their conduct, not by their professions.
— *Anon*

CONFESSION
I own the soft impeachment.
— *Sheridan, The Rivais*

There are some things which men confess with ease, but others with difficulty.
— *Epicuras, Discourse*

To confess a fault freely is the next thing to being innocent of it.
— *Syrus*

CONFIDENCE

Skill and confidence are an unconquered army.
— *George Herbert, Jacula Prunentum*

Trust not him that hath once broken faith.
— *Shakespeare*

They conquer who believe they can.
— *Dryden*

By mutual confidence and great discoveries made.
— *Homer, Illiad*

Self trust is the essence of heroism.
— *Emerson*

CONQUEROR

I came, I saw, conquered
— *Julius Caesar, Letter to Amaritus, 47 BC*

CONSCIENCE

Conscience is a sacred sanctuary where God alone may enter as a judge.
— *Lamennais*

Conscience is God's presence in man.
— *Swedenborg, Arcana Coelesta*

Love is too young to know what conscience is;
Yet who knows not conscience is shorn of love.
— *Shakespeare*

CONSENT

A little while she strove, and much repented,
And whispering 'I will ne'er consent, consented.
— *Byron, Don Juan*

CONSERVATIVE

A conservative is a man who is too cowardly to fight and too fat to run.
— *Elbert Hubbadr, Epigrams*

CONSIDERATION

Consideration is the soil in which wisdom may be expected to grow, and strength may be given to every upbringing plant of duty.
— *Emerson*

CONSISTENCY
A foolish consistency is the hobgoblin of little minds, adored by little statesmen and philosophers and divines.
— *Emerson, Essays : Self-Reliance*

CONSOLATION
There is no consolation in truth alone.
— *Pascal, On Death*

Over the bridge of sights we pass to the place of peace.
— *C.H. Spurgeon, 'Salt Cellar'*

CONSPIRACY
Conspiracies no sooner should be formed Than Executed.
— *Addison, Cato*

O conspiracy
Sham'st thou to show they dangerous brow by night
When evils are most free.
— *Shakespeare, Julius Caesar*

CONSTANCY
Constancy is the foundation of virtues.
—*Bacon, Du Augmentis Scientarlum*

The secret of success is constancy to purpose.
— *Disraeli*

CONSTITUTION
What's the Constitution between friends ?
— *Timothy J. Campbell, To pres. Cleveland, 1885.*

CONTEMPLATION
In order to improve the mind, we ought less to learn than to contemplate.
— *Descartes*

CONTEMPT
Grown all to all, from no one vice exempt
And most contemptible, to show contempt.
—*Pope, Moral Essays*

No one can boast of having never been despised.
— *Vauvangius, Maxims*

CONTENT

He that wants money, means and content, is without three good friends.
— *Shakespeare, As you Like It*

When we have not what we like, we must like what we have.
— *Bussy Rabutin, Letter to Mme. de Sevigne*

Sweet are the thoughts that savour of content.
The quiet mind is richer than crown.
— *R. Green, Farewell to Folly*

My soul hath her contents to absolute
That another comfort like this
Succeeds in unknown fate.
— *Shakespeare, Othello*

CONTEST

O, the more angle she
And you the blacker devil!
—*Butler—Hudibras*

CONTRADITION

Do I Contradict myself ?
Very well, then I contradict myself.
— *Walt Whitmen-Song of Myself*

Assertion is not argument, to contradict the statement of an opponent is not proof that you are correct.
— *Johnson*

CONTROVERSY

There is consolation in the fact that the controversies and in taking mineral waters, it is the after-effects that are real effects.
— *Schopenhauer, Dialogue on Religion*

CONVERSATION

Silence is one great art of conversation.
— *Hazlitt*

Conversation is the laboratory and workshop of the student.
— *Emerson*

Silence and modesty are very valuable qualities in conversation.
— *Montaique*

COQUETTE
There is only one antidote for coquetry and that is true love.
— *Madam Dehuzy*

CORRUPTION
O that estate, degrees, and offices were not purchased by the merit of the water!
— *Shakespeare*

COSMOPOLITAN
I am not an Athenian or a Greek, but a citizen of the world.
— *Scorates- (Quoted by Plutarch)*

COURAGE
The greatest test of courage on earth is to bear defeat without losing heart.
— *R.G. Ingersoll, The Declaration of Independence*

A man of courage is also full of faith.
— *Cicero*

COURTESY
Life is never so short, but there is always time for courtesy.
— *Emerson*

COURTS
A court is an assemblage of noble and distinguished beggars.
— *Tallyrand*

COURTSHIP
She half consents, who silently denies.
— *Ovid*

COVETOUSNESS
Refrain from covetousness and the estate shall prosper.
— *Plato*

Desire of having is the sin of covetousness.
— *Shakespeare*

COWARDICE
Cowards die many times before their death;
The valiant never tastes death but once.
— *Shakespeare, Julius Caesar*

The coward never on himself relies,
But to an equal for assistance flies.
— *George Grabbe, Tale in Verse*

CREDITOR
A creditor is worse than a master; for a master owns only your person, a creditor owns your dignity and can belabour that.
— *Victor Hugo, Les Miserables*

He that hath lost credit is dead to the world.
— *Herbert*

CREDULITY
Ye who listen with credulity to the whispers of fancy, and pursue with eagerness the phantoms of hope.
— *Samuel Johnson, Rasselas*

CREED
Orthodoxy is my doxy; heterodoxy is another man's doxy.
— *William Warburton, To Lord Sandwich*

CRIME
And who are the greater criminals than those who sell the instruments of death, or those who buy and use them ?
— *Robert E. Sherwood, Idiot's Delight*

Fear follows crime and is its punishment.
— *Voltaire*

Evil deeds are done for the mere desire of occupation.
— *Ammiamus Marcellinus, Historia*

Successful crimes alone are justified.
— *Dryden, The Medal*

CRISIS
These are the time that try man's souls.
— *Thomas Paine, The American Crisis*

CRITICISM
The good critic is he who narrates the adventure of his soul among masterpieces.
— *Anatole France, La Vie Litteraire*

Performance of one's duty should be independent of public opinion.
— *M. Gandhi*

CROSS
Under his standard shall thou conquer.
— *Emperor Constantine, Motto assumed by him*

CRUELTY
Of all beasts the man beast is the worst;
To others and himself the cruellest foe.
— *R. Bexter, Hypocricy*

I must be cruel, only to be kind.
— *Shakespeare, Hamlet*

Cruelty and fear shake hands together.
— *Balzac*

CULTURE
Culture is "to know the best that has been said and thought in the world."
— *Mathew Arnold, Literature and Dogma*

No culture can live if it attempts to be exclusive.
— *M. Gandhi, Harijan*

CUNNING
Satan's successes are the greatest when he appears with the name of God on his lips.
— *M. Gandhi, Young India*

CUPID
The wimpled, shining, purblind wayward by,
This senior-junior, giant dwarf, Dan cupid.
— *John Lyly, Alexander and Compaspe*

CURFEW
The curfew tolls the knell of parting day.
— *Gray, Flegy written in a Country Churchyard*

CURIOSITY
I loathe that low vice, curiosity
— *Byron*

Born in an age more curious than devout.
— *Young, Night Thoughts*

CURSE
>I shall curse you with book and bell and candle.
>— *Sir Thomas Malory, Morted' Arthur*

>Curses, not loud but deep.
>— *Shakespeare*

CUSTOMS
>Custom the world's great idol, we adore.
>— *J. Pomfret, Reason*

>Custom doth make dotards of us all.
>— *Carlyle*

>Custom is often only the antiquity of error.
>— *Cyprian*

CYNIC
>A man who knows the price of everything and the value or nothing.
>— *Osar Wilde, Lady Windermere's oan*

>Cynicism is intellectual dandyism.
>— *George Meredith, Egoists*

>To look upon life as an evil and treat the world as a delusion is sheer ingratitude.
>— *S. Radhakrishnan, Great Indians*

D

DANCING
Dancing, the child of Music and Love.
— *Sir John David, Orchestra*

Come, and trip it as you go.
On the light fantastic toe.
— *Milton, L. Allegre*

DARING
And darest thou then
To beard the lion in his den :
The Douglas in his hall :
— *Scott, Marinor*

DARKNESS
No light, But rather darkness visible.
— *Milton, Paradise Lost*

What is this unseen flame of darkness whose sparks are the stars.
— *Tagore, Stray Birds*

Night's darkness is bag that bursts with the gold of the dawn.
— *Tagore*

DAWN
The night kisses fading day whispering to his ear, "I am death, your mother. I am to give you fresh birth."
— *Tagore, Stray Birds*

DEAD
Marley was dead to begin with …… Old Marley was as dead as a door-nail.
— *Dickens, A Christmas Carol*

Let the dead bury their dead.
— *New Testament, Mathew*

DEATH

O' earth, where is thy sting? O grave, where is thy victory?
— *New Testament, Corinthions*

It is as natural to die as to be born.
— *Bacon, Essay on death*

The fountain of death makes the still waters of life play.
— *Tagore, Stray Birds*

Gone before, to that unknown and silent shore.
— *Lamb*

Heaven gives its favourities — early death.
— *Byron, Childe Harold*

Death is the golden key that opens the place of eternity.
— *Milton*

Be still prepared for death; and death of ill shall be the sweeter.
— *Shakespeare*

DEBT

He that dies pays all debts.
— *Shakespeare, Tempest*

The second vice is lying : the first is running into debt.
— *B. Franklin, Poor Richard*

DECEIT

O, what a tangled web we weave, when first we practise to deceive!
— *Walter Scott*

She has deceived her father, and may thee.
— *Shakespeare, Othello*

No man was ever so much deceived by another as by himself.
— *Greville*

DECISIONS

Let your yea be yea : and your nay, nay.
— *St. James, V. 12*

The woman that deliberates is lost.
— *Joseph Addison*

DECORUM
Nor will virtue herself look beautiful unless she be bedecked with the outward armaments of decency and decorum.
— *Fielding, Tome Jones*

DEEDS
Noble deeds that are concealed are most esteemed.
— *Pascal*

Think nothing done while aught remains to do.
— *Rogers, Human Life*

Good deeds ring clear through heaven like a bell.
— *Richier*

DEFEAT
I would rather suffer defeat than have cause to be ashamed of victory.
— *Quintus Curtius*

Defeat is a school in which truth always grows strong.
— *H.W. Beecher*

DEFENCE
The conquering cause was pleasing to the gods, but the conquered to Cato.
— *Lucan Pharasalia*

Millions of defence but not one cent for tribute.
— *Charles C. Pinkney*

DEFIANCE
He manned himself with dauntless air.
Returned the Chief his haughty stare.
— *Scott, Lady of the Lake*

DEGRADATION
A man that could look no way but downwards, with a muck rake in his hand.
— *Bunyah, Pilgrim's Progress*

DELAY
Defer no time; delays have dangerous ends.
— *Shakespeare*

Delay of justice is injustice.
— W.S. Landor, Du Play

In delay we waste our lights in vain : like lamps by day.
— Shakespeare

DELIBERATIONS
Take time enough; all other graces
Will soon fill up their proper places.
— Byron, Advice to Preach Show

DELICACY
Delicacy is to mind what fragrance is to the fruit.
— A. Poinoelot

DELIGHT
Life is not life at all without delight.
— Andrew Barten

The places delight where saints dwell whether in the village or in the forest; in deep water or on dry land.
— Sayings of Buddha

DELUGE
After us the deluge!
— Mme. De Pompadour, To Louis XV

DELUSION
To look upon life as an evil and treat the world as delusion is sheer ingratitude.
— S. Radhakrishnan, Great Indians

The disappointment of manhood succeeds the delusion of youth.
— Disraeli

I was never much displeased with those harmless delusions that tend to make us more happy.
— Goldsmith, Vicar of Wakefield

The worst deluded are the self-deluded.
— Bovee

DEMOCRACY
Government of the people, by the people, for the people.
— A. Lincoln

The devil was the first democrat.
> — *Byron*

The world must be made safe for democracy.
> — *Woodro Wilson*

Democracy will break under the strain of apron strings. It can exist only on trust.
> — *Mahatma Gandhi— Delhi Diary*

A born democrat is born disciplinarian.
> — *Mahatma Gandhi, Harijan*

DEPENDENCE
The great man living may stand in need of the meanest, as much as the meanest does of him.
> — *Fuller*

DENIAL
Suppression of woman is a denial of Ahimsa.
> — *Mahatma Gandhi, Harijan*

DEPARTURE
But, O the heavy change, now thou art gone.
Now thou art gone, and never must return!
> — *Milton, Lycidas*

DESCRIPTION
I feel, but want the power to paint.
> — *Juvenal*

DESERT
The mighty desert is burning for the love of a blade of grass who shakes her head and laughs and flies away.
> — *Tagore, Stray Birds*

DESIRE
There are two tragedies in life. One is not to get your heart's desire. The other is to get it.
> — *Barnard Shaw*

Our desire lends the colours of the rainbow to the mere mists and vapours of life.
> — *Tagore, Stray Birds*

He who desires naught will always be free.
— E.R. Lefebvre Laboulayn

We live in our desires rather than in achievements.
— George Moore

DESOLATION

My desolation begins to make a better life.
— Shakespeare

DESPAIR

What we call despair is often only the painful eagerness of unfed hope.
—George Eliot

O now, for ever
Farewell the tranquil mind farewell content.
— Shakespeare, Othello

DESPATCH

There is nothing more requisite in business than despatch.
— Addison, The Drummer

Despatch is the soul of business and nothing contributes more to despatch than method.
— Lord Chesterfield, Advice to his son

DESPERATION

Tempt not a desperate man.
— Shakespeare, King John

DESPONDENCY

Despondency is ingratitude; hope is God's worship.
— H.W. Beecher

DESPOTISM

Step by step and word by word; who is ruled may read.
Suffer not the old Kings — for we know the breed.
— Kipling, The Old Issue

DESTINY

This generation of Americans has a rendezvous with destiny.
— Franklin D. Roosevelt, Address, 1936

DESTRUCTION

Havoc, and spoil, and ruin are my gain.

— *Milton*

Where there is love there is life, hatred leads to destruction.

— *M. Gandhi*

The prerogative of destruction belongs solely to the Creator of all that lives.

— *M. Gandhi, Young India*

DETERMINATION

Tomorrow let us do or die!

— *Campbell, Gertrude*

DETRACTION

Let there be gall enough in thy ink; though thou write with a goose pen no matter.

— *Shakespeare, Twelfth Night*

Happy are they that hear their detractions, and can put them to mending.

— *Shakespeare*

DEVIATION

When people once begin to deviate they do not know where to stop.

— *George III*

DEVIL

The devil can cite scriptures for his purpose.

— *Shakespeare, Merchant of Venice*

He will give the devil his due.

— *Shakespeare, Henry IV*

DEVOTION

And all my fortunes at thy foot I'll lay,
And follow thee, my lord throughout the world.

— *Shakespeare, Romeo and Juliet*

All is holy where devotion kneels.

— *O.W. Holmes*

DEW
   Every dew-drop and rain-drop had a whole heaven within it.
   — *Longfellow*

DICE
   The best throw with the dice is to throw them away.
   — *Proverb*

DIET
   One meal a day is enough for a lion, if not to be for a man.
   — *C. Fordyce*

DICTATORSHIP
   .... the ultimate failures of dictatorship cost humanity far more than any temporary failures of democracy.
   — *Franklin D. Roosevelt, Address, 1937*

DIFFICULTY
   The greatest difficulties lie where we are not looking for them.
   — *Geothe*

DIFFIDENCE
   We are often duped by diffidence as by confidence.
   — *Chesterfield*

   Even with the best desert goes diffidence.
   — *Browning*

DIGNITY
   Perhaps the only true dignity of man is his capacity to despise himself.
   — *George Santayana, Introduction to Spinoza*

   No race can prosper till it learns that there is much dignity in tilling a field as in writing a poem.
   — *Broker T. Washington, Up From Slavery*

DIPLOMACY
   Diplomacy is to do and say the nastiest thing in the nicest way.
   — *Issac Goldberg*

DIPLOMAT
   Diplomat is a man who remembers a lady's birthday but forgets her age.
   — *Anon*

DIRT
Dirt is not dirt, but only something in the wrong place.
— *Lord Palmerston*

DISAPPOINTMENT
Disappointment is the nurse of wisdom.
— *Sir Boyle Boche*

As for disappointing them I should not so much mind; but I can't abide to disappoint myself.
— *Goldsmith, She Stoops to Conquer*

How disappointment tracks the steps of hope.
— *L.E. London*

DISASTER
Night was our friend; leader was despair.
— *Virgil, Aeneid*

DISCIPLINE
Discipline is learnt in the school of adversity.
— *M. Gandhi*

Silence is part of the spiritual discipline of a tary of truth.
— *M. Gandhi, Autobiography*

DISCONTENT
Discontent is the first step in the progress of a man or nation.
— *Oscar Wilde, Woman of No Importance*

Now is the winter of our discontent.
— *Shakespeare*

DISCOVERY
A new principle is an inexhaustible source of new views.
— *Vanvenargues*

DISCRETION
When you have got an elephant by the hind leg, and he is trying to run away, it's best to let him run.
— *Abraham Lincoln*

The better part of valour is discretion.
— *Shakespeare, Henry VI*

DISCUSSION
Understand your antagonist before you answer him.
— *Canning*

DISEASE
We classify disease as error, which nothing but Truth of Mind can heal.
— *Marry Barker Eddy, Science and Health*

DISGRACE
I cannot tell, good sir, for which of his virtues it was, but he was certainly whipped out of the court.
— *Shakespeare, Winter's Tale*

No one can disgrace us but ourselves.
— *J.G. Holland*

DISHONESTY
He who purposely cheats his friend, would cheat his God.
— *Lavoter*

DISHONOUR
The shame is in the crime not in the punishment.
— *Voltaire, Artemire*

DISMISSAL
I do desire we may be better strangers.
— *Shakespeare, As You Like It*

DISOBEDIENCE
Rogues differ little. Each began first as a disobedient son.
— *Chinese Proverb*

DISPARAGEMENT
With silent smiles of slow disparagement.
— *Tennyson, Guinever*

Of whom to be disappraised were no small praise.
— *Milton, Paradise Regained*

DISPATCH
Dispatch is the soul of business.
— *Chesterfield*

DISPLAY
The bost of heraldry, the pomp of power.
— *Gray, Elegy*

DISTANCE
Distance lends enchantment to the view.
— *T. Campbell, The Pleasure of Hope*

DISSIMILATION
The continual habit of dissimilation is but a weak and sluggish cunning, and greatly politic.
— *Bacon, Adv. of Learning*

DISTINCTION
He was a man, take him for all in all,
I shall not look upon his like again.
— *Shakespeare, Hamlet*

DISTRUST
What loneliness is more lonely than distrust ?
— *George Eliot*

Doubt the man who swears to his devotion.
— *Mme Louise Colet*

DIVINE
There is a divine purpose behind every physical calamity.
— *Mahatma Gandhi, Harijan*

DOCTOR
Physician, heal thyself.
— *New Testament, Luke IV*

DOCTRINE
Pure doctrine always bears fruit in pure benefits.
— *Emerson*

DOG
Do not disturb the sleeping dog.
— *Alexander Allegro*

A living dog is better than a dead lion.
— *Old Testament, Ecclesiastes*

DOING
Whatever is worth doing at all is worth doing well.
— *Chesterfield*

DOMESTICITY
In all the necessities of life there is not a grater plague than servants.
— *Gibber, She Would And She Would*

When in doubt, win the trick.
— *Hoyle*

DOVE
On that I had wings like a dove! For then would I fly away and be at rest.
— *Old Testament, Psalms*

DRAMA
Have you not perceived the tendency of your soul during comedy, how a mixture of pain and pleasure is found therein.
— *Plato, Philebus*

DREAMS
In the drowsy, dark caves of the mind, dreams built their nest and fragments dropped from day's caravan.
— *Tagore, Fireflies*

Dream is the wife who must talk, sleep is husband who silently suffers.
—*Tagore, Stray Birds*

Let not our babbling dreams affright our souls.
— *Shakespeare*

Children of the night, of indigestion bred.
— *Churchill*

DRESS
Eat to please thyself, but dress to please others.
— *Franklin*

She just dressed enough for modesty no more.
— *Robert Buchanan*

DRINKING

O God that men should put an enemy in their mouths to steal away their brains! that we should, with joy, pleasance, revel and applause, transform ourselves into beasts!
— *Shakespeare, Othello*

O thou invisible spirit of wine, if thou hast no means to be known by, let us call thee devil.
— *Shakespeare, Othello*

DRUNKENNESS

Habitual intoxication is the epitome of every crime.
— *Jerrols*

DUEL

A duellist is only a cain in high life.
— *Jerrols*

DUTY

Non-cooperation with evil is sacred duty.
— *M. Gandhi, Harijan*

Do thy duty which lies nearest thee, which thou knowest to be a duty ! The second duty will already become clearer.
— *Carlyle, Sartor*

The reward of one duty done is the power to fulfil another.
— *George Eliot*

DYING

Truth sits upon the lips of a dying man.
— *M. Arnold, Sohrah*

Oh, but they say the tongues of dying men enforce attention, like deep harmony.
— *Shakespeare, Richard II*

The art of dying bravely and with honour did not need any special training save a living faith in God.
— *M. Gandhi, Daily Diary*

E

EAGERNESS

I see you stand like grey hounds in the slips.
Straining upon the start.
— *Shakespeare, Henry V*

EARLY

Early to bed and early to rise
Makes a man healthy, wealthy and wise.
— *Franklin*

The early morning hath gold in its mouth.
— *Wellington*

EARNESTNESS

A man in earnest finds means, or if he cannot, creates them.
— *Canning*

EASE

For not to leave at ease is not to live.
— *Deyden, Persius*

Studious of laborious ease.
— *Cowper, The Garden*

EATING

The proof of the pudding is in the eating.
— *Cervantes*

Other men live to eat, while I eat to live.
— *Socrates*

Let us eat and drink; for tomorrow we shall die.
— *Old Testament, Isaiah*

ECCENTRICITY
That so few now dare to be eccentric marks the chief danger of the time.
— *J.S. Mill, Liberty*

ECHO
Our echoes roll from soul to soul,
And grow for ever, for ever.
— *Tennyson, The Princess*

ECONOMY
Ere you consult your fancy, consult your purse.
— *Franklin*

He who will not economize will have to agonize.
— *Confucius*

Beware of little expenses; a small leak will sink a great ship.
— *Franklin*

EDUCATION
Nothing in education is so astonishing as the amount of ignorance it accumulates in the form of inert facts.
— *Henry Adams, The Education of Henry Adams*

Education is the chief defence of nations.
— *Burke*

What then is education ? Surely gymnastics for the body and music for the mind.
— *Plato, Republic*

Education begins with life.
— *Franklin*

The great secret of education is to secure the body and mental exercise shall always serve that relax one another.
— *Rousseau, Emile*

EFFICIENCY
Wealth, power and efficiency are the appurtenances of life and not life itself.
— *S. Radhakrishnan, Great Indians*

One has to achieve not merely technical efficiency but greatness of spirit.
— *S. Radhakrishnan, Great Indians*

EFFORT
There is nothing which has not been better before being ripe.
— *Publius Syrus*

We must so strive that each man may regard himself as the chief cause of the victory.
— *Xeo phon*

EGO
Faith in conceptual reason is the logical counterpart of the egoism which makes the selfish ego the deadliest ego of the soul.
— *S. Radhakrishnan, Eastern Religions*

EGOISM
I find no sweeter fat that sticks to my own bones.
— *Walt Whitman, Song of Myself*

ELOQUENCE
He mouths a sentence as curs mouth a bone.
— *Churchill, Rosciad*

Thoughts that breathe and words that burn.
— *Gray*

Eloquence is the mistress of all the arts.
— *Tacitus, De Oratotibus*

EMINENCE
Censure is the tax a man pays to the public for being eminent.
— *Swift, Thoughts on Various Subjects*

EMPIRE
All empire is an immense egotism.
— *Emerson, The Young American*

All empire is no more than power in trust.
— *Absalom and Achitophel*

EMPLOYMENT
The hand of little employment hath the daintier sense.
— *Shakespeare, Hamlet*

EMULATION
Envy, to which the ignoble mind's slave,
Is emulation in the learned or brave.
— *Pope, Essay on Man*

ENCOURAGEMENT
All may do what by man has been done.
— *Young*

END
Let the end try the man.
All's well that ends well, still the finis is the crown.
— *Shakespeare*

ENDEAVOUR
We always succeed when we only wish to do well.
— *Rousseau, Emile*

Hard things are compassed oft by easy means.
— *Massinger, New Way to Pay Old Debts*

ENDINGS
There is an endless merit in man's knowing when to have done.
— *Carlyle, Francia*

ENDURANCE
He conquers who endures.
— *Presius*

ENEMIES
It is impossible for any man not to have some enemies.
— *Lord Chesterfield, Advice to His Son*

There is no little enemy.
— *Franklin*

ENERGY
Genius is mainly an affair of energy.
— *M. Arnold*

This world belongs to energetic.
— *Emerson*

The reward of a thing well done is to have done it.
— *Emerson*

ENJOYMENT
Only mediocrity of enjoyment is allowed to man.
— *Blair*

ENLIGHTENMENT
The shining light that shineth more and more upto the perfect day.
— *Proverb*

Human nature is fundamentally good, and the spread of enlightenment will abolish all wrong.
— *S. Radhakrishnan, Eastern Religion and Western Thoughts*

ENMITY
Enmities always keep pace and are interwoven with friendship.
— *Plutarch, On Friendship*

ENTERPRISE
Kites rise against not with the wind — no man ever worked his passage anywhere in a dead claim.
— *John Neal*

ENTERTAINMENT
For one of the pleasures of having a rout
Is the pleasure of having it over.
— *Hood, Kilmansegg*

ENTHUSIASM
The enthusiasm of old men is singularly like that of infancy.
— *Nerval*

Nothing great was achieved without enthusiasm.
— *Emerson, Circles*

ENTHUSIAST
The prudent man may direct state, but it is the enthusiast who regenerates it or ruins.
— *Lord Lytton, Rienzi*

ENVY
Envy has no other quality but of detracting from virtue.
— *Livy*

The most anti-social and obvious of all passions, envy.
— *J.S. Mill, Liberty*

It is better to be envied than pitied.
— *Herodotus*

EPICURES

He hath a fair sepulchre in the grateful stomach of the judicious epicure and for such a tomb might content to die.
— *Lamb, Roast Pig*

Let's go hand in hand, not one before another.
— *Shakespeare*

EQUALITY

A good judge judges according to what is right and good, and prefers equity to strict law.
— *Coke*

EQUIVOCATION

The cruellest lies are told in silence.
— *R.L. Stevenson, Virginibus*

I doubt the equivocation of a friend that lies like truth.
— *Shakespeare, Macbeth*

ERROR

Error is the force that welds men together; truth is communicated to men only by deeds of truth.
— *Tolstoy, My Religion*

To err is human, To persist in error is devilish.
— *S. Augustine, Sermon*

ESTEEM

All true love is founded on esteem.

Buckingham

ETERNITY

Nothing is there to come, and nothing past,
But an eternal now does always last.
— *Cowley, Garened*

Evil and good are God's right and left.
— *Bailey*

ETIQUETTE

Where etiquette prevents me from doing things disagreeable to myself, I am a perfect martinet.
— *Sydney Smith, Letter to Lady Holland*

EVENING
The day is done, and the darkness falls from the wings of Night.
— *Longfellow, Day is Done*

EVENTS
I claim not to have controlled events, but confess plainly that events have controlled me.
— *Abraham Lincoln*

Coming events cast their shadows before.
— *Campbell*

These most brisk and giddy-paced time.
— *Shakespeare*

EVIDENCE
Some circumstantial evidence is very strong : as when you find a trout in the milk.
— *H.E. Thoreau, Unpublished Mss.*

The ear is less trustworthy witness than the eye.
— *Herodotus*

EVIL
The evil that men do lives after them;
The good is oft interred with their bones.
— *Shakespeare, Julius Caesar*

It is a great evil not to be able to bear an evil.
— *Bion*

Evil by itself has no legs to stand upon
— *Mahatma Gandhi, Harijan*

Evil to him who evil thinks.
—*Motto of The Order of the Garter*

EVOLUTION
The survival of the fittest, which I have here sought to express in mechanical terms, is that which Mr. Darwin has called 'natural selection', or the preservation of favoured races in the struggle for life.
— *Herbert Spencer, Principles of Biology*

Evolution is not the force but a process, not a cause but a law.
— *Lord Morley, Compromise*

EXAMPLE
Nothing is so infectious as example.
— *Charles Kingsley*

Example is lesson that all men can read.
— *Gilbert West*

EXCELSIOR
Fearless minds climb soonest upon crowns.
— *Shakespeare*

EXCESS
The best things carried to excess are wrong.
— *Churchill, Rosciad*

EXPERIENCE
Experience keeps a dear school, yet Fools will learn in another.
— *Franklin, Poor Richard's Almanac for 1743*

A sadder and a wiser man.
He rose the morrow morn.
— *S.T. Coleridge*

EXPLANATION
I wish he would explain his explanation.
— *Byron, Don Juan*

EXPRESSION
The language of the soul never lends itself to expression. It rises superior to the body. Language is a limitation of the truth which can only be represented by life.
— *Mahatma Gandhi, Harijan*

EXTRAVAGANCE
Extravagance and good luck, by long custom, go hand in hand.
— *Madame D. Arblay, Camilla*

Waste of time is the most extravagant and costly of all expenses.
— *Theophratus*

EXTREMES
Avoid extremes.
— *Clecobulus of Lindes*

Excess of sorrow laughs, excess of joy weeps.
— *Wm. Blake, Proverbs of Hell*

Neither great poverty nor great riches will hear reason.
— *Fielding*

EYES

The eyes believe themselves; the ears believe other people.
— *German Proverb*

We must look the world in the face with calm eyes even though the eyes of the world are bloodshot today.
— *Mahatma Gandhi*

F

FACE

Man is read in his face.
— *Ben Johnson*

A cheerful face is merely as good for an invalid as health weather.
— *Franklin*

Your face is a book, where men may read strange matters.
—*Shakespeare*

FACTION

Party is the madness of many for the gain of the few.
— *Pope, Miscellanies*

FACTS

Get your facts, and then you can distort them as you please.
— *Mark Twain, Interview*

FAILINGS

And even his failings leaned to virtue's side.
— *Goldsmith, Deserted Village*

FAILURES

There is not a fiercer hell than the failure in a great object.
— *Keats, Pref. to Endymion*

But to him who tries and fails and dies, I give great honour and glosy and tears.
— *Joaquim Miller*

FAITH

They went forth to battle, but they always fell.
— *Macphfrson, Cath-loda*

If you have faith in the cause and the means and in God, the hot sun will be cool for you.
— *Mahatma Gandhi, The Epic of Travancore*
Faith is the continuation of reason.
— *William Adams*
Work without faith is like an attempt to reach the bottomless pit.
— *Mahatma Gandhi*

FAITHFULNESS
The deepest hunger of a faithfull heart is faithfulness.
— *Eliot, Spanish Gypsey*

FALL
Dropped from the zenith like a fallen star.
— *Milton*
How art thou fallen from heaven, O Lucifer, son of the morning !
— *Old Testament, Isaiah*
How are the mighty fallen!
— *Old Testament, II Samuel*

FALLIBILITY
We are none of us infallible, not even the youngest.
— *W.H. Thompson*

FAME
Passion for fame : a passion which is the instinct of all great souls.
— *Burke, Speech on American Taxation*
Fame is the perfume of heroic deeds.
— *Socrates*
What a heavy burden is a name that has become famous.
— *Voltaire*
I awoke one morning and found myself famous.
— *Byron, Children Harold*

FAMILIARITY
Familiarity breeds contempt and children.
Familiarity is a magician that is cruel to beauty but kind to ugliness.

FAMILY

All happy families resemble one another : every unhappy family in its own way.

— *Tolstoy, Anna Karenina*

FAREWELL

For ever, brother, hail and farewell.

— *Catullus, Old*

Fare thee well and if for ever,
Still for ever, fare thee well.

— *Byron, Fare Thee Well*

FARMER

All farmers fatten most when famine reigns.

— *S. Garth, Dispensary*

Slave of the wheel of labour, what to him.
Are Plato and the swing of Pleiades.

— *Edwin Markham, The Man with the Hoe*

A farmer is always going to be rich next year.

— *Philemon*

FASCINATION

He hath a smooth dispose
To be suspected; framed to make woman false.

— *Shakespeare, Othello*

FASCISM

National socialism does not harbour the slightest aggressive intent towards any European nation.

— *Adolf Hitler, Nazi Congress 1939*

FASHION

While the world lasts, fashion will continue to lead it by the nose.

— *Cowper*

I see that the fashion wears out more apparel than the man.

— *Shakespeare*

FASHIONABLE

A fashionable woman is always in love with herself.

— *La Rochefoucauld*

FASTIDIOUSNESS
Fastidiousness is the envelope of indelicacy.
— Haliburton

FASTING
Fasting is futile unless it is accompanied by an incessant longing for self-restraint.
— Mahatma Gandhi

FATALITY
As killing as the canker to the rose.
— Milton, Lycidas

FATE
With patience bear, with prudence push, your fate.
— Virgil, Aeneid

Tempted fate will leave the loftiest star.
— Byron

We make our fortunes and we call them fate.
— Disraeli

FATHER
Father : to Go Himself we cannot give.
A holier name.
— Wordsworth, Lord Ullin's Daughter

FAULT
A fault confessed is half redressed.
— H.G. Bohn

The greatest of fault, I should say, is to be conscious of none.
— Carlyle, Heroes and Hero-Worship

FAVOURS
Extreme eagerness to return an obligation is a kind of ingratitude.
—Roche Foucauld

FEAR
Let us fear God and we shall cease to fear man.
— Mahatma Gandhi, Speeches and Writings

In time we hate which we often fear.
— Shakespeare

Early and provident fear is the mother of safety.
— Burke

FEASTS
The true essential of a feast are only fun and feed.
— O.W. Holmas, Nux Postvoenatics

He who feasts every day, feasts no day.
— C. Simmon

FELLOWSHIP
Write me as one that loves his fellow men.
— Leigh Hunt, Abou Ben Adhem

If he be not fellow with the best king.
Thou shalt find the best King of good fellows.
— Shakespeare, Henry V

FEELINGS
There for some feelings time cannot be numb.
— Byron, Child Harold

He who has felt nothing does not know how to learn anything.
— Rousseau, Juliet

FEES
If money goes before, always doors lie open.
— Shakespeare, Merry Wives of Windsor

FERVOUR
No wild enthusiast ever yet could rest,
Till half mankind were like himself possessed.
— Cowper, Progress of Error

FICKLENESS
The uncertain glory of an April day.
— Shakespeare

FICTION
Literature is luxury, fiction is a necessity.
— G.K. Chesterton, The Defendent

Man is a poetical animal and delights in fiction.
— Hazlitt

FIDELITY
>Fidelity is the sister of justice.
>> — *Horace*

>I will follow thee
>To the last gasp with truth and loyalty.
>> — *Shakespeare, As You Like It*

FIGHT
>I have not yet begun to fight.
>> — *John Paul Jones*

>There is such a thing as a man being too proud to fight.
>> — *President Wilson, Speech 1915*

>For a fighter the fight itself is victory for he takes delight in it alone.
>> — *Mahatma Gandhi, Satyagraha in South Africa*

FINALITY
>What's done is done.
>> — *Shakespeare, Hamlet*

FINANCE
>The fact is, the moment financial stability is assured, spiritual bankruptcy is also assured.
>> — *Mahatma Gandhi, 70th Birthday Volume*

>Public credit means the contracting of debts which a nation never can pay.
>> — *W. Cobbett, Advice to Young Men*

FIRE
>A burnt child dreads the fire.
>> — *Ben Johnson*

>Better a little fire that warms than a big one that burns.
>> — *John Ray*

FIRMNESS
>It is only those who possess firmness who can possess true gentleness.
>> — *Law Rochefoucauld, Maxim*

>When firmness is sufficient, rashness is unnecessary.
>> — *Napoleon*

FLAG
The imperial ensign, which full high advanced, Shone like a meteor, streaming to the wind.
— *Milton, Paradise Lost*

FLATTERY
Flattery corrupts both the receiver and the giver.
— *Burke, Reflections on the Revolution*

One catches more flies with a spoonful of honey with twenty casks of vinegar.
— *Henry IV of France*

It is easy to flatter, it is harder to praise.
— *Jean Paul Richter*

FLESH
The word, the flesh, and the devil.
— *Book of Common Prayer*

The spirit indeed is willing, but the flesh is weak.
— *New Testament, Mathew*

FLIRTATION
What we find the least of in flirtation is love.
— *Milton, Paradise Lost*

FLOWERS
Full many a flower is born to blush unseen,
And waste its sweetness on the desert air.
— *Gray*

Let us crown ourselves with rosebunds before they be withered.
— *Wisdom of Soloman*

But I will woo the dainty rose, the queen of every one.
— *Hood, Flower*

FLY
The fly sat upon the axle-tee to the chariot wheel, said, "What a dust do I raise!"
— *Francis Bacon, Essays*

The wanton body that kills a fly, Shall feel the spider's enmity.
— *Blake*

FOLLY
There is a foolish corner even in the brain of a sage.
— *Aristotle*

He who lives without folly is not so wise as he imagines.
— *Rochefoucauld*

FOOL
None but a fool is always right.
— *J.C. Hare, Guesses at Truth*

My flower, seek not thy paradise in a fool's buttonhole.
— *Tagore, Fireflies.*

Let a fool be made serviceable according to his folly.
— *Joseph Conrad, Under Western Eyes.*

What fools these mortals be!
— *Shakespeare, A Midsummer Night's Dream*

FOOL'S PARADISE
Into a Limbo large and broad, since call'd.
The Paradise of Fools, to few unknown.
— *Milton, Paradise Lost*

FOOT
Her feet beneath her petticoat.
Like little mice, stole in and out,
As if they feared the light.
— *Suckling, Ballad Upon a Wedding*

FORCE
Everyday preserves in its state of rest or uniform motion in a straight line, except in so far as it is compelled by the change that state by impressed forces.
— *Isaac Newton, Principia*

What is readily yielded to courtesy is never yielded to force.
— *Mahatma Gandhi*

Force is rugged way of making love.
— *S. Butler, Cat and Pus.*

FOREBODING
Knowing how Nature threatens ere she springs.
— *R. Buchanam, Meg Blane*

FORECAST
O that man might know.
The end of this day's business ere it come!
— *Shakespeare, Troilus*

FORETHOUGHT
In life, as in chess forethought wins.
— *Buxton*

Fore-warned fore-armed.
— *Miguel De Cervantes*

FORGIVENESS
Forgiveness adorns a soldier.
— *Mahatma Gandhi, Young India*

Forgive us our debts, as we forgive our debtors.
— *New Testament, Luke*

The heart has always the pardoning power.
— *Madame Swetchine*

Nobody ever forgets where he buried hatchet.
— *Kin Hubbard, Abe Martin's Broadcast*

FORMALITY
In general, the more completely cased with formulas a man may be safer, happier it is for him.
— *Carlyle, Past and Present*

FORTUNE
Fortune never seems to blind as to those upon whom she has bestowed no favours.
— *La Rochefoucauld, Maxims*

Every man is the architect of his own fortune.
— *Mme Dorothy Keluzy*

We make our own fortunes, and call them fate.
— *Alroy*

FRANKLIN BENJAMIN
I succeed him; no one could replace him.
— *Thomas Jefferson, On Being Made Envoy to France*

FRANKNESS
There is no wisdom like frankness.
— *Disraeli, Sytil*

FRAUD
The first and worst of all frauds is to cheat oneself.
— *Bailey*

FREEDOM
None can love freedom heartily but good men; the rest love not freedom, but licence.
— *Milton, Tenure of Kings*

We gain freedom when we have paid the full price for our right to live.
— *Tagore, Fireflies*

A man who is made for freedom has got to take tremendous risk and take everything.
— *Mahatma Gandhi*

The cause of freedom is the cause of God.
— *Samuel Bowles*

FREE WILL
Sufficient to have stood, though free to all.
— *Milton, Paradise Lost*

FRIEND
Love is only chatter
Friends all that matter
— *Gelet Burgess, Willy and the Lady*

FRIENDSHIP
Change your pleasure, but do not change your friends.
— *Voltaire, La Depositaire*

Most friendship is freigning, most loving mere folly.
— *Shakespeare, As You Like It*

There are three faithfull friends : an old wife, an old dog and ready money.
— *Franklin*

Adversity is the crucible in which friendship is tested.
— *Mahatma Gandhi, Young India*

FROWNS
Full well the busy whisper, circling round, conveyed the dismal tiding when he frowned.
— *Goldsmith, Deserted Village*

FRUGALITY
By sowing frugality we reap liberty, a golden harvest.
— *Agesilasus*

Overjoyed was he to find,
That though she was on pleasure, bent
She had a frugal mind.
— *Cowper, John Cilpin*

FRUITS
Though to her things grow fair against the sun,
Yet fruits that blossom first will first be ripe.
— *Shakespeare, Othello*

FURY
Beware the fury of a patient man.
— *Dryden, Absalom and Achitophel*

FUTURE
I never think of the future. It comes soon enough.
— *Albert Einstein, Interview 1939*

Ignorance of future ills is a more useful thing than knowledge.
— *Cicero, De Div*

When all else is lost, the future still remains.
— *Bovee*

The highest wisdom is never to worry about the future but to reign ourselves entirely to His will.
— *Mahatma Gandhi, Harijan*

G

GAIETY

Gaiety is often the reckless ripple over depths of despair.
— *E.H. Chapin*

GAIN

Gain cannot be made without some other person's loss.
— *Pubilious Syrus*

Sometimes the best gain is to lose.
— *Herbert*

GALLANTRY

So faithfull in love and so dauntless in war.
There never was knight like the young Lochinvar.
— *Scott, Marmion*

GAMBLING

There are two times in a man's life when he should not speculate; when he can't afford it and when he can.
— *Mark Twain, Pudd'nhead Wilson Calendar*

Keep flax from fire and youth from gambling.
— *Franklin*

It is the child of avarice, the brother of inequity, and the father of mischief.
— *George Washington*

Gambling is a principle inherent in human nature.
— *Burke, Speech on Economical Reform*

GAMES

The game is not worth the candle.
— *Montaigne, Essay*

It is not shameful to have played games, but it is shameful not to have left of playing them.

— *Horace Epistles*

GARDEN

The best place to seek God is in a garden. You dig for Him there.

— *G.B. Shaw, Adventures of the Black Girl*

God the first Garden made, and the first city Cain.

— *Gawley*

God Almighty first planted a garden; and indeed it is the purest of human pleasures.

— *Bacon, Of Gardens*

GENERALITIES

General notions are generally wrong.

— *Lady M. Morley Mantagu, Letter*

General and abstract ideas are the source of the greatest of man's errors.

— *Rousseau, Emile*

GENEROSITY

My beauty is as bountiless as the sea,
My love as deep.

— *Shakespeare, Romeo and Juliet*

There was a man, though some did think him mad.
The more he cast away, the more he had.

— *Bunyan, Pilgrim's Progress*

GENIUS

Genius is nothing but a great aptitude for patience.

— *Buffon*

Genius is infinite painstaking.

— *Longfellow, To Revenue Officers in America*

Spiritual life is the genius of India.

— *S. Radhakrishnan, Great Indians*

Great genius have the shortest biographies.

— *Emerson*

Genius must be born, it can never be taught.

— *Dryden*

GENTILITY
How weak a thing is gentility, if it wants virtue.
— *Fuller*

GENTLEMAN
There is no character which a low-minded man so much mistrusts as that of a gentleman.
— *Thackeray, Vanity Fair*

When Adam delved and Eve span
Who was then the gentleman ?
— *John Ball*

GENTLENESS
Your gentleness shall force
More than your force to move us to gentleness.
— *Shakespeare, As You Like It*

Nothing is strong as gentleness : nothing so gentle as real strength.
— *Francis De Sales*

GHOST
I am thy father's spirit,
Doom'd for a certain time to walk the night.
— *Shakespeare, Hamlet*

All argument is against it but all belief is for it.
— *Johnson*

On the Appearance of Men's Spirits after Death.

GIANT
There were giant in the earth in those days.
— *Old Testament, Genesis*

GIFT
I make presents to the mother, but think of the daughter.
— *Goethe*

For gifts are scorned where givers are despised.
— *Dryden, Hind and Panther*

For to the noble mind.
Rich gifts wax poor, when givers prove mankind.
— *Shakespeare, Hamlet*

GIRL
Men seldom make passes.
At girls who wear glasses.
— *Dorothy Parker, News Item*

What are little girls made of? Sugar and spice and all things nice.
— *Southey*

An unlessoned girl, unschooled, unpractised.
— *Shakespeare, Merchant of Venice*

GLORY
Glory follows virtue like its shadow.
— *Cicero*

What Price Glory?
— *Maxwell Anderson*

Like madness is the glory of this life.
— *Shakespeare*

The nearest way to strive to glory is to be what you wish to be thought to be.
— *Socrates*

Glory lies in the attempt to reach one's goal and not reaching it.
— *M. Gandhi, Harijan*

GOD
God is incorporal, divine, supreme, infinite.
Mind, Spirit, Soul Principal, Life, Truth, Love.
— *Mary Baker Eddy, Science and Health*

A foe to God was never true friend to man.
— *Young*

God is not a cosmic bell-body for whom we can press a button to get things.
— *Harry Emerson, Prayer*

Fear that man who fears not God.
— *Abdel Kader*

God's great power is in the gentle breeze not in the storm.
— *Tagore*

God is truth and light is shadow.
— *Plato, The Republic*

If God did not exist, it would be necessary to invent him.
— *Voltaire*

GOD
O love of gold ! thou meanest of amours !
— *Edward Young, Night Thoughts*

Thou gaudy gold.
Hard good for Midas.
— *Shakespeare, Merchant of Venice*

Every door is barred with gold, and opens but to golden keys.
— *Tennyson, Locksley Hall*

GOLDEN RULE
Therefore all things whatsoever ye would that should do unto you; do ye even so unto them.
— *New Testament, Mathew*

The golden rule is that there is no golden rule.
— *Bernard Shaw, Maxims of Revolutionists*

GOOD
Good breeding is surface Christianity
— *G.W. Holmes*

'Tis only noble to be good.
— *Tennyson, Lady Clara Vere de Vere*

I defy the wisest man in the world to turn a truly good action into ridicule.
— *Fieldind, Joseph Andrews*

Be good and you will be lonesome.
— *Mark Twain, M. Gandhi, Harijan*

GOOD AND BAD
Abhor that which is evil ! cleave to that which is good.
— *New Testament*

GOSSIP
Pitchers have ears, and I have many servants.
— *Shakespeare, Taming of the Shrew*

It is the folly of too many to mistake the echo of a London coffee-house for the voice of the kingdom.
— *Swift, Conduct of the Allies*

Foul whisperings are abroad.
— *Shakespeare*

GOVERNMENT
Government of the people, by the people, for the people.
— *Abraham Lincoln, Gettysburg Address*

The safety of the State is the highest law.
— *Justinian*

Every country has the Government it deserves.
— *Joseph De Maister*

No government can possibly withstand the bloodless opposition of a whole nation.
— *Mahatma Gandhi*

GRACE
You are a fallen from grace.
— *Galatians*

Such easy greatness, such a graceful port
So turned and finished for the camp or court.
— *Addison, Campaign*

The word 'Grace' in an ungracious muck is profane.

GRAMMAR
Why care for grammar as long as we are good !
— *Artemus, Ward, Pyrotechny*

For all your rhetorician's rules.
Teach nothing but to name his tools.
— *Butler, Hubbiras*

GRAPES
The fathers have eaten sour grapes and the children's teeth are set on edge.
— *Old Testament, Ezekiel*

GRATITUDE
Gratitude is the memory of the heart.
— *J.B. Massieu*

Though the thorn in thy flower pricked me.
O Beauty,
I am grateful.
— *Tagore, Fireflies*

Gratitude is a lively sense of future favours.
— *Sir Robert Walpole*

GRAVE
Grave is but the threshold of eternity.
— *Southey*

There the wicked cease from troubling, and there the weary be at rest.
— *Old Testament, Job*

The house that he makes last till the doomsday.
— *Shakespeare*

GREATNESS
Man becomes great exactly in the degree in which he works for the welfare of his fellowmen.
— *Mahatma Gandhi, Ethical Religion*

Greatness and goodness are not means, but ends.
— *Coleridge, Job's Luck*

All great men come out of middle classes.
— *Emerson*

The great are only great because we are on our knees. Let us rise.
— *P.J. Proudhon, Revolution of Paris*

What millions died that Caesar might be great.
— *Compbel*

He is not great who is not greatly good.
— *Shakespeare*

GREECE
Achilles' warth, Greece the direful spring.
Of woes unnumbered, heavenly Goddess, sing !
— *Homer, Iliad*

GREEKS
I fear the Greeks, even when bringing gifts.
— *Virgil, Aeneid*

GRIEF
Grief is itself a medicine.
— *Cowper, Charity*

Every one can master a grief but he that has it.
— *Shakespeare*

Sorrow's best antidote is employment.
— *Young*

No grief is so acute but time ameliorates it.
— *Cicero*

GRUMBLE

It is a general popular error to suppose the loudest complaints for the public to be the most anxious for its welfare.
— *Burke, Observation on Present of Nations*

Those who complain most are most to be complained of.
— *M. Henry*

GUEST

A pretty woman is a welcome guest.
— *Byron, Bepps*

Pleasantest of all ties is the tie of host and guest.
— *George W. Resse*

Be right and jovial among your guests tonight.
— *Shakespeare*

The friendship laws are by this rule expressed.
Welcome the coming, speed the parting guest.
— *Pope, Odyssey*

GUILT

Guilt is always jealous.

Hearty repentance broke the edge of guilt and led the way to a proper understanding.
— *Mahatma Gandhi, Delhi Diary*

Every man carries the bundle of his sins,
Upon his own back.
— *John Fletcher, Rule a Wife*

H

HABIT
Habit with him was all the test of truth;
'It must be right : I've done it from my youth.
— *George Grebbe*

Ill habits gather by unseen degrees.
As brooks make rivers run into seas.
— *Dryden, Tr. Ovid*

Habit is ten times nature.
— *Wellington*

The fox changes his skin but not his habits.
— *Suetonius*

Great is the force of habit; it teaches us to bear labour and to scorn injury and pain.
— *Cicero*

HAIR
How ill white hair become a fool and a jester.
— *Shakespeare*

My hair is grey, but not with years.
Nor grew it white,
In a single night,
As men's have grown with sudden fears.
— *Byron, The Prisoner of Chillon*

HANDS
Pale hands I loved beside the Shalimar,
Where are you now ? Who lies beneath your spell ?
— *Laurence Pope, Kashmir Song*

There is no better sign of a brave mind than a hard hand.
— *Shakespeare, Henry VI*

All the perfumes of Arabia will not sweeten this little hand.
— *Shakespeare, Macbeth*

Let us go hand in hand, no one before another.
— *Shakespeare*

HANGING
We must all hang together, else we shall hang separately.
— *Benjamin Franklin*

HAPPENINGS
Yet sometime it shall fall on a day
That falleth not oft within a thousand year.
— *Chaucer, Knight's Tale*

HAPPINESS
Happiness depends on what you can give, not what you can get.
— *Mahatma Gandhi, Young India*

That action is best which procures the greatest happiness for the greatest numbers.
— *Francis Huchinson, An Inquiry into Beauty and Virtue*

Happiness lies, first of all, in health.
— *George William Curts*

How wide the limits stand.
Between a splendid and a happy land.
— *Goldsmith, Deserted Village*

The best secret of happiness is renunciation.
— *Andrew Carnegie*

The happy only are the truly great.
— *Young, Love of Fame*

Now the heart is so full that a drop overfills it.
We are happy now because God will it.
— *J.R. Lowell, The Vision of Sir Launfal*

HARD-HEARTEDNESS
Worse than a bloody hand in a hard heart.
— *Shelly, Cenci*

HARDNESS
Plenty and peace breeds cowards; hardness ever hardness is mother.
— *Shakespeare*

HARDSHIP
Ability and necessity dwell near each other.
— *Pythagorus*

HARM
Who dare harm whom God protects ?
— *Mahatma Gandhi, Autobiography*

HARMONY
Heard melodies are sweet, but those unheard are sweeter.
— *Keats, On A Gercian Urn*

HARP
We hanged our harps upon the willows.
— *Old Testament-Psalms*

HASTE
Haste administers all things badly.
— *Statius, The Baidos Libri*

Haste is of the devil.
— *Koran*

Hurry is the mark of a weak mind : despatch of a strong one.
— *C.C. Colton, Lacon*

Make haste slowly.
— *Emperor Augustus*

HATE
Hate is the subtlest form of violence.
— *Mahatma Gandhi, Harijan*

Hating people is like burning down your own house to get rid of a rat.
— *Harry Emerson, The Wages of Haste*

Hated by fools, and fools to hate,
By that my motto and my fate.
— *Swift, To Dr. Delany*

All our world organisations will prove ineffective if the truth that love is stronger than hate does not inspire them.
— *S. Radhakrishnan, Great Indians*

HATRED

People hate as they love : unreasonably.
— *Thakeray*

Hatred is a settled anger.
— *Cicero*

To instruct the human race need one discard humanity ?
It is the torch of hatred indispensable to show us the truth ?
— *Voltaire, Fanaticism*

In time we hate that we often fear.
— *Shakespeare*

Hatred is self punishment.
— *Housaballon*

HEAD

Two heads are better than one.
— *Proverb*

And still they gaz'd and still the wonder grew.
That one small head could carry all he knew.
— *Goldsmith, The Deserted Village*

HEALTH

A sound mind in a sound body is a thing to pray for.
— *Juvenal*

The first wealth is health.
— *Emerson*

Early to bed and early to rise,
Makes a man healthy, wealthy and wise.
— *Franklin*

Every day, in every way, I am getting better and better.
— *Emile Coue*

Give me health and a day I will make the pomp of emperors ridiculous.
— *Emerson, Inspiration*

HEART

The heart has no language; it speaks to the heart.
— *Mahatma Gandhi, Among The Great*

My heart is turned to stone : I strike it, and it strikes my hand.
— *Shakespeare*

Hands cling to hands and eyes linger on eyes, thus begins the record of our hearts.
— *Tagore, The Gardener*

A good heart is worth gold.
— *Shakespeare*

The heart of the fool is in his mouth, but the mouth of the wise man is in his heart.
— *Franklin, Poor Richard's Almanac*

Kind hearts are more than coronets
And simple faith than normal blood.
— *Tennyson, Lady Clara Vere de Vere*

There is no instinct like that of the heart.
— *Byron*

O hearts that break and give no sign
Save whitening lips and facing tresses.
— *O.W. Holmes, The Voiceless*

Where your treasure three will your heart be also.
— *New Testament, Luck*

HEAVEN

In my father's house are many mansions.
— *New Testament, John XIV*

All this, and heaven too !
— *Philip Henry*

Earth has no sorrow that heaven cannot heal.
— *Moore*

The love of heaven makes one heavenly.
— *Shakespeare*

And I saw a new heaven and a new earth; for first heaven and the first earth were passed away : and there was no more sea.
— *New Testament, Revolution*

HECUBA

What's Hecuba to him or he to Hecuba ?
— *Shakespeare, Hamlet*

HELL
Wide is the gate and broad is the way that leadeth to destruction and many there be which go in threat.
— *New Testament, Mathew*

The loss of heaven's the greatest pain in hell.
— *Sir S. Tucke, Adv. of Five Hours*

The gates of hell are open night and day;
Smooth the decent and easy is the way,
— *Virgle, Aeneid*

HELP
Sweet the help of one we have helped.
— *Homer*

Light is the task where many share the toil.
— *Homer*

God helps us when we feel ourselves humbler than the dust under our feet. Only to the weak and helpless is divine succour vouchsafed.
— *Mahatma Gandhi, 70th Birthday Volume*

HEN
A hen is only an egg's way of making another egg.
— *Samuel Butler, Life and Habit*

HEREDITY
Few sons attain the praise,
Of their great sires, and most their sires disgrace.
— *Pope, Odyssey*

A worthy son always adds to the legacy that he receives.
— *M. Gandhi, Harijan*

HERESY
Better heresy of doctrine than heresy of heart.
— *Whitter, Mary Carvin*

HERO
One murder makes a villian : million a hero.
— *Porteus*

Heroes have trod this spot — 'tis on their dust ye breed.
— *Byron, Childe Harold*

Give honour to our heroes fall'n, how ill
Soe'er the cause that bade them forth to die.
— William Watson, *The English Dead*

No men is a hero to his own wife;
No one women is a wife to her hero.
— Anon

No man is a hero to his valet.
— Madame De Coranuel

HERO-WORSHIP
A highbrow is a person educated beyond his intelligence.
— Brander Matthews, *Epigrams*

HESITATION
When we are in doubt whether an action is good or bad, abstain from it.
— Zoroaster, *Maxim*

HISTORY
The prophets of spirit make history just by standing outside history.
— S. Radhakrishnan, *Great Indians*

The history of the world is the record of a man in quest of his daily bread and butter.
— H.W. Van Loon, *The Story of Mankind*

We read history through our prejudices.
— Wondell Philips

History in bunk
— Henry Ford

The men who make history have no time to write it.
— Matternich

Happy are the people whose annals are tedious.
— Motesquieu

What is history but a fable agreed upon ?
— Napolean Bonaparte, *Sayings*

Assassination has never changed the history of the world.
— Disraeli

Man's history is waiting in patience for the triumph of the insulted man.
— Tagore, *Stray Birds*

All history is lie.

— *Sir Robert Walpole*

History is something that never happend, written by a man wasn't there.

— *Anon*

HOLIDAY

If all the year was playing holiday, to sport would be as tedious as to work.

— *Shakespeare*

What is this life, full of care,
We have no time to stand and stare ?

— *W.H. Davies*

HOLY

Holiness is the summetry of the soul.

— *Philip Henry*

A holy man is one who never considers himself superior to any single creature on earth and who has renounced all the pleasures of life.

— *Mahatma Gandhi*

HOME

Home is where the heart is.

— *Pliny*

Home is the place where, when you have to go there.
They have to take you in.

— *Robert Frost, The Death of the Hired Man*

A comfortable house is a great source of happiness. It ranks immediately after health and good conscience.

— *Letter to Lord Murray*

Type of the wise, who soar, but never roam — True to the kindred points of Heaven and Home.

— *Wordsworth, To a Skylark*

Without heart there is no home.

— *Byron*

HOMER

Seven cities warred for Homer, being dead,
who, living, had no roof to shroud his head.

— *Thomas Heywood, On Homer's Birthplace*

HONESTY

Honesty is the best policy.
— *Franklin*

Honesty is really only the art of a peering honest.
— *Guarini, Of the Honesty or Virtue of Women*

An honest man's the noblest work of God.
— *Pope, Essay on Man*

No legacy is so rich as honesty.
— *Shakespeare*

A straight line is shortest in morals as well as in geometry.
— *Rahel*

Only the man of serene mind can realise the spiritual meaning of life. Honesty with oneself is the condition of spiritual integrity.
— *S. Radhakrishnan*

HONOUR

I could not love thee Dear, so much.
Lov'd I do not honour more.
— *Lovelace, To Lucasta*

We honour the illustrious dead best by following their example.
— *M. Gandhi, Harijan*

If I lose mine honourable, I lose myself.
— *Shakespeare*

What is fitting is honour; what is honourable is fitting.
— *Cicero*

HONOURS

Honours and great employment are great burdens.
— *Massinger, Bondman*

HOPE

Hope springs in the human breast,
Man never is, but always to be blest.
— *Pope, Essay on Man*

For where no hope is left, on fear.
— *Milton, Paradise Regained*

HOPELESSNESS
I cultivate hope and I see it wither daily; Alas, what does it serve to water the leaves when the tree is cut off at its foot.
— *Rousseau, Juliet*

HORRORS
Farewell happy fields.
Where joy for ever dwells ! Hail horrors hail !
— *Milton, Paradise Regained*

HORSE
A horse ! a horse ! my kingdom for a horse !
— *Shakespeare, Richard III*

You may lead a horse to water but you can't make him drink.
— *Proverb*

A horse thou knowest, a man thou does not know.
— *Tennyson*

HOSPITALITY
I was a stranger, and ye took me in.
— *Mathew, New Testament*

On hospitable thoughts intent.
— *Milton, Paradise Lost*

HOUSE
I in my own house am an emperor,
And will defend what's mine.
— *Roman Actor, Massinger*

The house of every one is to him his castle and fortress, as well for his defence against injury and violence, as for his repose.
— *Sir Edward Coke*

HUMANITY
After all there is but one race-humanity.
— *George Moore*

I am a man, and nothing human can be of indifference.
— *Terence, The self Torturer*

Real education consists in drawing the best of yourself; What better book can there be than the book of humanity.
— *Mahatma Gandhi*

But hearing often times.
The still and music of humanity.
— *Wordsworth, Tintern Abbey*

HUMBLE
...'umble we are, 'umble we have been, 'umble we shall ever be.
— *Dickens, David Copperfield*

HUMILITY
Humility is the key to quick success.
— *M. Gandhi, Young India*

Humility is the root, mother, nurse, foundation, and bend of all virtues.
— *Chrysostom*

Whatsoever shall smite thee on the right cheek, turn to him the other also.
— *Mathew, New Testament*

Be lowly, wise;
Think only what concerns thee and thy being; Dream not of other words.
— *Milton, Paradise Lost*

HUMOUR
If I had no sense of humour, I should long ago have committed suicide.
— *M. Gandhi*

Good humour is one of the best articles of dress one can wear in society.
— *Thackeray*

HUNGER
The best sauce for food is hunger.
— *Socrates*

HUNTING
When a man wants to murder a tiger, he calls it sport; when a tiger wants to murder him he calls it ferocity.
— *G.B. Shaw, Maxims for Revolutionists*

HYPOCRISY

No man is a hypocrite in his pleasures.
— *S. Johnson*

False face must hide what the false heart doth know.
— *Shakespeare*

A man is at his worst when he pretends to be good.
— *Publius Syrus*

I

IDEAL
An ideal is that which never touches the real.
— *Schiller, To Goethe*
He is the greatest artist who has embodied in the sum of his works, the greatest number of greatest ideals.
We build statues of snow and weep to see them melt.
— *Sir Walter Scott*
When a man works for an ideal, he becomes irresistible.
— *M. Gandhi, Young India*

IDEALIST
An idealist is a person who helps other people to be prosperous.
— *Henry Ford*

IDLENESS
Go to the ant, thou sluggard, consider her way, and be wise.
— *Old Testament, Proverb*
Idleness is only the refuge of weak mind.
— *Earl of Chesterfield, Letter to His Son*
Lost time is never gained again.
— *Aughey*
Of all our passions the one we are least cognizant of its idleness.
— *La Rochefoucauld, Maxims*
There is no greater cause of melancholy than idleness.
— *Burton, Anatomy of Melancholy*
I loaf and invite my soul.
I lean and loaf at my ease observing a spear of summer grass.
— *Walt Whitman, Song of Myself*

IDOLS
Four species of idols best the human mind : idols of the tribe; idols of the den; idols of the market; idols of the theatre.
— *Francos Bacon, Nevum Organum*

IF
Your 'if' is the only peace-maker : much virtue in 'if'.
— *Shakespeare, As You Like It*

IGNORANCE
There is no darkness but ignorance.
— *Shakespeare, Twelfth Night*

Better be unborn than untaught, for ignorance is the root of misfortune.
— *Plato*

I am not ashamed to confess that I am ignorant of what I do not know.
— *Cicero*

Where ignorance is bliss, 'Tis folly to be wise.
— *Gray*

ILL
We trust that somehow good will be the final goal of ill.
The surest way to health, say what they will,
Is never to suppose we shall be ill.
— *C. Churchile, Night*

ILLUSION
So does the glory depart, and so dangerous and disillusioning is it to grow up.
— *F.V. Lucas, One Day and Another*

IMAGINATION
Were it not for imagination, Sir a man would be as happy in the arms of chambermaid as of a Duchess.
— *S. Johnson*

Imagination is the eye of the soul.
— *Joubert*

Don't let us make imaginary evils, when you know we have so many real one's to encounter.
— *Goldsmith, Good-natured Mane*

Imagination rules the world.
— *Napoleon*

The faculty of degrading God's work which man calls his "imagination".
— *Ruskin, Modern Painters*

IMITATION
Imitation is the sincerest of flattery.
— *C.C. Gotton,*

Imitation belittles.
— *Bovee Lacon*

We imitate only what we believe and admire
— *Willmot*

And the man who plants cabbages imitates too !
— *Austin Dobson*

IMMORTALITY
The seed dies into new life, and so does man.
— *G. Macdonald*

Dust thou art, to dust returnest.
Was not spoken of the soul.
— *Longfellow, A Pslam of life*

Immortality will come to such as are fit for it, and he who would be a great soul in future must be a great soul now.
— *Emerson, Conduct of Life*

I wish to believe immortality—I wish to live with you for ever.
—*Keats*

What is a human is immortal.

IMPATIENCE
Impatience dries the blood sooner than age of sorrow.
— *Cleon*

IMPERFECTION
He censures God who quarrels with the imperfection of men.
— *Burke*

The best of what we do and are.
Just God, forgive
— *Wordsworth*

IMPERIALISM
In every part of the world the good desire of men for peace and decency is undermined by the dynamic of jingoism. And it needs only one spark, set off anywhere by the egomaniac, to end it all up in one final fatal explosion.
— *Robert E. Sherwood, Idiot's Delight*

IMPOSSIBILITY
You write "it is not possible". That is not French.
— *Nepolean*

Few things are impossible to diligence and skill.
— *Samuel Johnson*

A wise man never attempts impossibilities.
— *Masslnger, Renegado*

IMPRESSIONABILITY
I am a part of all that I have met.
— *Tennyson, Ulysses*

IMPROMPTU
Impromptu is truly the touch stone of wit.
— *Moliere, Less Prieuses*

IMPROVEMENT
The spirit of improvement is not always a spirit of liberty; for it may aim at forcing improvement on an unwilling people.
— *J.S. Mill, Liberty*

Much of a wisdom of one age is folly of the next.
— *C. Simmons*

People seldom improve when they have no other model but themselves to copy after.
— *Goldsmith*

IMPROVIDENCE
Waste not, want not; wilful waste makes woeful want.
— *Franklin*

IMPUDENCE
Bold knaves thrive, without one grain of sense.
But good men starve for want of impudence.
— *Dryden*

For be that has but impudence.
To all things has a just pretence.
— *S. Butler, Miscellaneous Thoughts*

IMPULSIVENESS
The pupil of impulse, it forced him along,
His conduct still right, with his argument wrong.
— *Goldsmith, Retaliation*

INACTION
An idle as a painted ship
Upon a painted ocean.
— *Coleridge, Ancient Mariner*

INACTIVITY
The mightiest powers deepest calms are fed.
— *B.w. Proctor*

INCONSTANCY
Clocks will go on as they are set : but man, irregular man is never constant, never certain.
— *Otway*

INDECISION
No man, having put his hand to the plow, and looking back, is fit for the Kingdom of God.
— *Lake, New Testament*

It is a miserable thing to live in suspense, it is the life of a spider.
— *Swift*

INDEPENDENCE
In the end injustice produces independence.
— *Voltaire*

Independence, like honour, is a rocky island without a beach.
He travels the fastest who travels alone
— *Kipling, The Winners*

Sink or swim, live or die, survive or perish, I give my heart and hand to his vote.
— *Daniel Webster*

INDICTMENT
I do not know a method of drawing up an indictment against whole nation.
— *Edmund Burke*

INDIFFERENCE
Full of sweet indifference.
— *R. Buchanant, Chairman*

INDIGNITIES
It can never be
They will digest this harsh indignity.
— *Shakespeare, Love's Labour Lost*

INDIVIDUALISM
Literary history and all history is a record of the power of minorities, and of minorities alone.
— *Emerson, Progress of Culture*

INDOLENCE
Indolence is the sleep of mind.
— *Valvenargus*

Self-restraint and not indulgence must be regarded as the law of life.
— *M. Gandhi, Self, Restraint*

INDUSTRY
Temperance and industry are the two real physicians of mankind.
— *Rawseau, Emile*

INEQUALITY
What are we ? How unequal ! Now we soar
And now we sink.
— *Young, Nights Thoughts*

INEVITABLE
No niggardly acceptance of the inevitable will appear pleasing to God.
— *M. Gandhi, Young India*

INFAMY
Leaving behind them horrible dispraise.
— *Dante, Infernot*

INFANCY
Heaven lies about us in our infancy.
— *Wordsworth*

INFANT
At first the infant,
Mewling and puking in the nurse's arms.
— *Shakespeare, As You Like It*

INFLUENCE
Canst thou bind the sweet influence of the Pleiades, or loose the bands of Orion ?
— *Old Testament, Job*

Let him that would move the world first move himself.
—*Socrates*

Influence is the exhalation of character.
— *M.W. Taylor*

How sharper than a serpent's tooth it is,
To have a thankless child !
— *Shakespeare, King Lear*

The goods received, the river is forgotten.
— *Congereve, To Lord Halifax*

Brutes leave ingratitude to man.
— *Colton*

INHUMANITY
No greater shame to man than inhumanity.
— *Spencer*

INHIBITION
Inhibitions imposed from without rarely succeed, but when they are self-imposed, they have decidedly salutary effect.
— *M. Gandhi, Autobiography*

INJURY
It is a principle of human nature to hate those whom you have injured.
—*Tautus*

No man is hurt but by himself.
— *Diogenes*

INJUSTICE
Unjust rule never endures perpetually.
— *Senea, Medea*

The most complete injustice is to seem just, when not so.
— *Plato, Republic*

INK
A drop of ink may make a million think.
— *Byron*

My ways are as broad as the king's high road, and my means lie in an inkstand.
— *Southy*

INNOCENCE
Innocence under an evil Government must ever rejoice on the scaffold.
— *M. Gandhi*

They that know no evil will suspect none.
— *Ben Johnson*

There is no courage but in innocence.
No constancy but in an honest cause.
— *T. Southern, Fate of Capua*

INNOVATIONS
Striving to better, oft we mar what's well.
— *Shakespeare*

INQUISITIVENESS
Avoid a person who asks questions, for such a man is a talker : nor will open ears keep faithfully the things entrusted to them.
— *Horace*

INSANITY
All power of fancy over reason is a degree of insanity.
Though this be madness, yet there is method in't.
— *Shakespeare*

INSENSITIVE
No one who holds himself aloof form the activities of the world and who is insensitive to its woes can be really wise.
— *S. Radhakrishnan, Great Indians*

INSINCERITY
Nothing is more disgraceful than insincerity.
— *Cicero*

The hearts of old gave hands :
But our new heraldry is ...... hands not hearts.
— *Shakespeare, Othello*

INSPIRATION
Great thoughts, great feelings come to him, like instincts, unawares.
— *Lord Boughtod*

There is God within us, and we glow when He stirs us.
— *Ovide, Fast*

No man was ever great without a touch divine afflatus.
— *Cicero*

INSTABILITY
He who begins many things finishes nothing.
— *C. Simmon*

INSTINCT
Instinct and reason how can we divide ?
'Tis' the fool's ignorance and the pedant's pride.
— *Prior*

INSTRUCTION
It is always safe to learn, even from our enemies, seldom safe to venture to instruct, even our friends.
— *C.C. Colton, Lacon*

INSULTS
An injury is much sooner forgotten than an insult.
— *Lord Chesterfield*

If you speak insults, you shall also hear them.
— *Plantes*

Insults are like bad coins : we cannot help their being offered to us but we need not take them.
— *G.H. Spurgeon, Salt Cellers*

INTEGRITY
Integrity is praised and starves.
— *Juvenal*

A man of integrity will never listen any plea against conscience.
— *Home*

An honest man's the noblest work of God.
— *Pope, Essay on Man*

INTELLECT
The power least prized is that which thinks and feels.
— *Wordsworth, Humanity*

All the wise...... therein really extolling themselves agree that Mind is to us a king of heaven and of earth.
— *Plato, Philebus*

Intellect obscures more than it illumines.
— *Zangwill*

INTELLIGENCE
Light has spread and even bayonets think.
— *Kossuth*

INTELLIGENT
Simplicity of character is no hindrance to subtlety of intellect.
— *John Viscount Morley*

No task's too steep for his wit.
— *Horace*

INTEMPERANCE
He that is a drunkard is qualified for all vice.
— *Quarlles*

INTEREST
The virtues and vices are all put in motion by interest.
— *Rochefoucauld*

INTOLERANCE
And when religious sects ran mad, he held in spite of all his learning.

Intolerance is itself a form of violence and an obstacle to the growth of a true democratic spirit.
— *Mahatma Gandhi*

INTUITION
A woman's intuition has often proved truer than man's arrogant assumption of knowledge.
— *M. Gandhi, Young India*

INVENTION
God hath made men upright, but they have sought out many inventions.
— *Old Testament*

Necessity is the mother of invention
— *Anon*

The devil has a very inventive mind.
— *Voltaire*

INVINCIBLE
I may be a despicable person but when truth speaks through me I am invincible.
— *M. Gandhi, The Epic Fast*

INVITATION
Whether they give or refuse, it delights women equally to have been asked.
Look with what courteous acting,
It waves you to a more removed ground.
— *Shakespeare, Hamlet*

IRRITATION
There is a common saying that when a horse is rubbed on the gall, he will kick.
— *Bishop Latimer*

IRISH
The Irish are the cry-babies of the Western world, Even the mildest quip will set them off into resolutions and protests.
— *Heywood Brown, The piece That Got Me Fired*

IVY
Oh, dainty paint is the Ivy green.
Teat creepeth o'er ruins old I
— *Dickens, The Ivy Green*

J

JEALOUSY

Nor jealously
Was understood, the injured lover's hell.
— *Milton, Paradise Lost*

I can endure my own despair.
But not another's hope.
— *William Walst, Song*

He that is not jealous is not in love.
— *St. Augustine*

JEST

The right honourable gentleman is indebted to his memory for his jests and to his imagination for his facts.
— *R.B. Sarridan*

JESTER

Alas; poor Yorich! I knew him, Horatio; a fellow of infinite jest, most excellent fancy.
— *Shakespeare, Hamlet*

JESTING

It is good to make a jest but not to make a trade jesting.
— *Fuller*

Take heed of jesting : many have been ruined by it.
— *Fuller*

The jests of the rich are ever successful.
— *Goldsmith, Vicar of Wakefield*

JEW

A race prone to superstition, opposed to religion.
— *Tacitus*

Hath not a Jew eyes ? Hath not a Jew hands, organs, dimensions, senses, affections, passions ?
— *Shakespeare, Merchant of Venice*

JEWEL
Rich and rare were the gems she wore,
And a bright gold ring on her hand she bore.
— *Moore, Irish Melodies*

JILTED
Better be courted and jilted.
Than never be courted at all.
— *Campbell, Jilted Nymph*

Say what you will, 'its better to be left, than never to have been loved.
— *Cong, Way of the World*

JOURNALISM
Great is Journalism. Is not every able Editor a Ruler of the World, being a persuader of it ?
— *Carlyle, French Revolution*

I fear three newspapers more than a hundred thousand bayonets.
— *Napoleon*

Journalism always says what they know is untrue in the hope that if they go on saying it long enough it will come true.
— *A Bennett, The Tile*

Get your facts first then you can distort them as you please.
— *Mark Twain*

JOY
Great joys, like griefs, are silent.
— *S. Marmion, Hollands Leaguer*

A thing of beauty is a joy for ever.
— *Keats*

There is a sweet joy that comes to us after sorrow.
— *Supergeon*

Joy is the battle. The result comes by the grace of God.
— *M. Gandhi, Harijan*

And joy, whose hand is ever at his lips. Bidding adieu.
— *Keats*

JUDAS
    And while he yet spoke, lo, Judas, one of the twelve came ... and forthwith he came to Jesus, and said Hail ! Master; and kissed him.
    — New Testament, Mathew

JUDGE
    Be your own judge and will be happy.
    — M. Gandhi
    Ordained of God to be the judge of quick and dead.
    — New Testament
    Thieves for their robbery have authority, when judges steal themselves.
    — Shakespeare

JUDGMENT
    O judgment ! thou art fled to brutish beasts.
    And men have lost their reason !
    — Shakespeare, Julius Caesar III
    Judgment is forced on us by experience.
    — Johnson

JUDGING
    To perceive is to feel; to compare is to judge.
    Judging and feeling are not the same thing.
    — Rousseau

JUDGMENT DAY
    God will not look you over for medals, degrees or diplomas, but for scars.
    — Alburt Hubbard, Epigrams
    Flee from the wrath to come.
    — New Testament, Mathew

JURY
    And hungry judges soon the sentence sigh.
    And wretches hang that jurymen may die.
    — Pope, The Rape of the Lock

JUSTICE
    Justice without generosity, may easily become Shylock's Justice.
    — M. Gandhi, Harijan

God's mill grinds slow, but sure.
— *George Herbert*

Live and let live is the rule of common justice.
— *Sir Roger, L' Estrange*

My experience has shown me that we win justice quickest by rendering justice to the other party.
— *M. Gandhi, Autobiography*

The administration of justice is the firmest pillar of government.
— *George Washington*

K

KINDNESS

Kindness gives birth to kindness.
— *Sophocles*

Kindness noble ever than revenge.
— *Shakespeare, As You Like It*

Little deeds of kindness, little words of love
Help to make earth happy, like the heaven above.
— *Jalia A. Carney, Little Things*

'Twas a thief said the last kind word to Christ :
Christ took kindness, and forgave the theft.
— *R. Browning, The Ring and the Book*

Kindness is the golden chain by which society is bound together.
— *Geothe*

KINDRED

A little more than kin, and less than kind.
— *Shakespeare*

KINGS

Kings are like stars—they rise, they set, they leave,
The worship of the world, but to repose.
— *Shelley*

A king of shreds and patches.
— *Shakespeare, Hamlet*

Kings and their swords are inferior to the swords of ethics.
— *M. Gandhi*

The power of kings (if rightly understood) is but a grant from Heaven of doing good.
— *W. Somerville*

KISSES

And our spirit rushed together at the touching of lips.
— *Tennyson*

Stolen kisses are always sweetest.
— *Leigh Hunt*

Leave a kiss but in the cup
And I'll not look for wine :
— *Ben Johnson, To Celia*

"Are you too proud to kiss me?" the morning light asks the butter cup.
— *Tennyson*

O a kiss,
Long as my exile, sweet as my revenge;
— *Shakespeare, Coriolanus*

Oh, fire, Miss, you must not kiss and tell.
— *Congreve, Love for Love*

KNAVE

The worst of all knaves are those who can mimic their former honesty.
— *Lavater*

Gainst knave and thieves men shut their gate.
— *Shakespeare, Twelfth Night*

KNEE

The human knee is joint and not an entertainment.
— *Percy Hammond*

KNIGHT

He then that is not furnished in this sort.
Doth but usurp the sacred name of knight.
— *Shakespeare, Henry VI*

He was a very perfect gentle knight.
— *Chaucer, Canterbury Tales*

KNOWLEDGE

Knowledge is power.
— *Hobbes*

Time and industry produce every day new knowledge.

— *Hobbes*

As for me, all I know is that I know nothing.

— *Socrates*

All I know is what I read in the papers.

— *Will Rogers*

L

LABELS
Don't rely too much on labels.
For too often they are fables.
— *C.H. Spurged*

LABOUR
Toil is the lot of all, and bitter woe.
The fate of many.
— *Homer, Iliad*

Honest labour bears a lovely face.
— *Dekker, Patient Grissel*

A man's best friend are his ten fingers.
— *Robert Collyer*

For as labour cannot produce without the use of and, the denial of the equal right to the use of land is necessarily the denial of the right of labour to its own product.
— *Henry George, Progress and Poverty*

Labour makes us insensible to sorrow.
— *Cicero*

Never work without reward, or reward without work.
— *Livy, Hist*

Without labour nothing prospers.
— *Sophocles*

What profit hath a man of all his labour which he taketh the sun?
— *Old Testament, Ecclesiastes*

LABOURER
The labourer is worthy of his hire.
— *New Testament*

A nation may do without his millionairs and without its capitalists but a nation can never do without its labourers.
— *M. Gandhi*

The labourer is worthy of his reward.
— *Timothy*

LARK

Hark, hark ! the lark at heaven's gate sings,
And phoebus' gins arise.
— *Shakespeare, Cymberline*

LANGUAGE

Music is the universal language.
— *John Wilson*

In the commerce of speech use only coins of gold and silver.
— *Joubert*

Language is the dress of thought.
— *Johnson*

One great use of words is to hide our thoughts.
— *Voltaire*

Language as well as the faculty of speech, was the immediate gift of God.
— *Webster*

LATENESS

Too late, too late ! ye cannot enter now.
— *Tennyson*

LAUGH

And if I laugh at any mortal thing,
'Tis that I may not weep.
— *Byron, Don Juan*

And the loud laugh that spoke the vacant mind.
— *Goldsmith, The Deserted Village*

Laugh if you are wise.
— *Mertial*

He laughs best who laughs last.
— *Proverb*

The burden of self is lightened when I laugh at myself.
— *Tagore, Fireflies*

LAUGHTER

Man is the only creature endowed with the power of laughter.
— *Greville*

Sport that wrinkled care derides
And Laughter holding both sides.
— *Milton*

As the cricking of thorns under a pot, so is the laughter of the fool.
— *Old Testament, Ecclesiastes*

Our sincerest laughter with some pain is fraught.
— *Shelly, To Skylark*

LAW

Mercy loosens the law.
— *Publius Syrus*

Laws govern the poor, and rich rule the law.
— *Goldsmith, The Traveller*

In law nothing is certain but the expense.
— *S. Butler*

Good laws are produced by bad customs.
— *Macrobius*

What is a law if those who make it become the forwardest to break it.
— *J. Beatie*

One of the laws is the law.
— *Walter Scott*

LAWYER

Necessity has no law; I know some attorneys of the same.
— *Franklin*

The true function of lawyer is to unite parties driven as under.
— *M. Gandhi, Life and Works*

A true lawyer is one who places truth and service in the first place and the emolument of the profession in the next place only.
— *M. Gandhi, Harijan*

LEADERSHIP
If the blind leads the blind, both shall fall into the ditch.
— Mathew

Here's to the pilot that weathered the storm.
— G. Canning, The Pilot

A leader is best when people barely know that he exists.
— Witter Byner

And when we think we lead we most are led.
— Byron

LEARNING
A little learning is a dangerous thing :
Drink deep, or taste not the Pierian spring :
— Pope, Essay on Criticism

Learning makes most men more stupid and foolish than they are by nature.
— Schopehauer, Thinking of Oneself

It is always in season for old man to learn.
— Aeschylus

A reformer who if enraged because his message is not accepted, must retire to the forest to learn how to watch, wait and pray.
— Mahatma Gandhi

LEISURE
Leisure is the time for doing something useful.
— Dr. N. Howe

Days of respite are golden days.
— South

A poor life this, if full of care,
We have no time to stand and stare.
— W.H. Davies, Leisure

Leisure in its activity is work.
The stillness of the sea stirs in waves.
— Tagore, Stray Birds

LENDING
Very often he that his money lends,
Loses both his gold and his friends.
— C.H. Spurgeor, John Ploughman

Neither a borrower nor a lender be :
For loan loses both itself and friend.
— *Shakespeare*

LETTER
Letter-writing : that most delightful way of wasting time.
— *Viscount Morley, Life of Geo Eliot*

The letter killeth; but the spirit giveth life.
— *New Testament, Corinthanis*

It is by the benefit of letters that absent friends are, in a manner, brought together.
— *Seneca*

LEVELLERS
Your levellers wish to level down as far as themselves; but they cannot bear levelling up to themselves.
— *Johnson, Remark*

LIAR
This is the punishment of a liar : He is not believed even when he speaks the truth.
— *Babylonian Talmud, Sanhedrin*

LIBEL
It often happens that if a lie be believed only for an hour, it has done its work and there is no further occasion for it.
— *Swift, Examiner*

LIBERTY
When liberty is gone,
Life grows insipid and has lost its relish.
— *Addison, Cato*

Burn the liberties, for their value it is this one book.
— *Caliph Omer*

Eternal vigilance is the price of liberty.
— *Jawaharlal Nehru, Broadcast*

The true University of these days is a collection of books.
— *Carlyle, Heroes and Hero Worship*

LIE
Sin has many tools, but a lie is the handle which fits them all.
— *Holmes*

Ask me no question and I'll tell you no fibs,
— *Goldsmith, She Stoops to Conquer*

LIFE

To enjoy life one should give up the lure of life.
— *Mahatma Gandhi, Harijan*

Is life worth living ? That depends on the liver.
— *Anon*

There should be limit even to the means to keeping ourselves alive. Even for life itself we may not require certain things.
— *M. Gandhi, Autobiography*

Human life as we have it is only the raw material for human life as it might be.
— *S. Radhakrishnan*

Life is made up of sobs, suffles, and smiles, with sniffles predominating.
— *O. Henry*

Life is long if you know how to use it.
— *Seneca*

Life is not a spectacle of feast : it is a predicament.
— *Santayana*

Welcome, O life ! I go to encounter for the millionth time the reality of experience and to forge in the smithy of my soul the uncreated conscience of my race.
— *James Joyce*

Life is real ! life is earnest !
And the grave is not its goal.
— *Longfellow, Psalm of Life*

LIGHT

Light is the shadow of God.
— *Plato*

Thanks the flame for the light, but do not forget the lamp holder standing in the shade with contractor and patience.
— *Tagore, Stay Birds*

Light is the symbol of truth.
— *J.R. Lowell*

Where there is light, there is also shadow.
— *M. Gandhi, Hind Swaraj*

I am the life of the world.
— *New Testament*

Hali holy light, offspring of Heav'n firstborn !
— *Milton, Paradise Lost*

LILY
Consider the lilies of the field, how they grow; they toil not, neither do they spin ! And yet I saw unto you, that even Solomon in all his glory was not arrayed like one of these.
— *New Testament, Mathew*

LINCOLN ABRAHAM
Now he belongs to the ages.

His heart was great as the world, but there was no room in it to hold the memory of wrong.
— *Emerson*

We are coming, Father Abraham, three hundred thousand more.
— *J.S. Gibbons*

LIPS
Lips, however rosy, must be fed.
— *Cheals*

LISTENERS
Give us grace to listen well.
— *Keble, Palm Sunday*

LITERATURE
Literature always anticipates life. It does not copy it, but moulds it to its purpose.
— *Oscar Wilde, The Decay of Lying*

Literature is the thought of thinking souls.
— *Carlyle*

Literature—the most seductive, the most deceiving, the most dangerous of professions.
— *Lord Morley*

Literature is the orchestration of platitudes.
— *Thorn Ton Wilder, Literature*

LIVE
Plain living and high thinking are no more.
— *Wordsworth*

LOGIC
He owns here logic of the heart, and reason of unreason.

LOOK
Cheerful looks make every dish a feast, and that it is which crowns a welcome.
— *Messinger*

LOQUACITY
You cram these words into my ears against the stomach of my sense.
— *Shakespeare*

LORD
The fear of Lord is the beginning of wisdom.
— *Old Testament*

The Lord is my light and my salvation.
— *Old Testament, Psalms*

LOSE
The man who can fight to Heaven's one height is the man who can fight when he's losing.
— *Service*

LOSS
Why do you make us love your godly gift. And snatch them straightaway ?
— *Shakespeare*

Wise men never sit and wail their loss.
— *Shakespeare*

LOVE
Love's the noblest frailty of the mind.
— *Dryden, Indian Emperor*

It's love, that makes the world go ground.
— *Anon*

Do not seat your love upon a precipice because it is high.
— *Tagore, Stray Birds*

He who does not come to the temple gate, he who loves reaches the shrine.
— *Tagore, Fireflies*

Love is the business of the idle, but the idleness of the busy.
— *Bulwar Lytton, Rienzi*

Love gives itself; it is not brought.
— *Longfellow*

LOVER

Love is blind, and lovers cannot see the pretty follies they themselves commit.
— *Shakespeare*

A lover without indiscretion is no lover at all.
— *T. Hardy*

And the lover, sighing like furnace, with a woeful ballad, made to his mistress's eyebrow.
— *Shakespeare, As You Like It*

LUCK

Good luck befriend thee, Son : for at thy birth,
The fairy ladies danced upon the hearth.
— *Milton*

Shallow men believe in luck. Strong men believe in cause and effect.
— *Emerson*

Call me not foot till heaven hath sent me fortune.
— *Shakespeare, As You Like It*

Happiness or misery generally go to those who have most of the one of the one or the other.
— *La Rochefoucauld*

LUST

The conquest of lust is the highest endeavour of a man's or woman's existence. Without overcoming lust man cannot hope to rule over self.
— *M. Gandhi, Harijan*

LUXURY

On the soft beds of luxury most kingdoms have expired. The superfluous — a very necessary thing.

— *Voltaire*

LYING

Lying is the mother of violence.

— *M. Gandhi, Young India*

Let me have no lying : it becomes non but tradesmen.

— *Shakespeare, Winter's Tale*

M

MADNESS
Though this be madness, yet there is method in it.
— *Shakespeare, Hamlet*

O, that way madness lies; let me shun that !
— *Shakespeare*

There is pleasure sure
In being mad, which none but mad men know.
— *Dryden*

MAGNANIMITY
The eagle suffers little birds to sing.
And is not careful what they mean thereby.
— *Shakespeare*

MAIDEN
The blushing beauties of a modest maiden.
— *Dryden*

The spinsters and the knitters in the sun.
And the free maids that weave their thread with bones.
— *Shakespeare, Twelfth Night*

MAMMON
Ye cannot serve God and Mammon.
— *New Testament*

MAN
I am seeking a man.
One cannot be always a hero, but one can always be man.
— *Goethe*

No man is as great as mankind.
— *Theodore Parker*

123

Men are not angels, neither are they brutes,
Something we may see, all we cannot see.

— *Browning*

For ours is a most fictile world and man is the most fingent plastic of creatures.

— *Carlyle*

MAN AND WOMAN

One among a thousand have I found; but a woman among all those have I not found.

— *Old Testament, Ecclesiastes*

MANLINESS

Manliness consist in making circumstances subservient to ourselves.

— *M. Gandhi, Young India*

MANNERS

What time ! What manners !

— *Gicero*

Men make laws; women make manners.

— *De Segur*

Everyone's manners make his fortune.

— *Cornelius Nepos*

MARRIAGE

To marry once is a duty, twice a folly, thrice a madness.

— *Proverb*

Marriage is the great civilizer of the world.

— *Robert Hall*

A good marriage would be between a blind wife and a deaf husband.

— *Montaigne, Essays*

Though women are angels, yet wedlock's the devil.

— *Byron, Hours of Idleness*

A young man married is a man that's married.

— *Shakespeare, All's Well that Ends Well*

A deaf husband and a blind wife are always a happy couple.

— *Proverb*

Don't thou marry for munny but goa wheer munny is.
— *Tewyson*

Alas ! another instance of the triumph of hope over experience.
— *Johnson*

MARTYRDOM
Let us all be brave enough to die the death of a martyr but let no one lust for martyrdom.
— *M. Gandhi, Young India*

It is the cause, not the death, which makes the martyr.
— *Napoleon*

MASTER
Find out, if you can,
Who's master, who's man.
— *Swift, My Lady's Lamentation*

Men at some time are masters of their fates.
— *Shakespeare*

No man can serve two masters.
— *New Testament, Mathew*

MEANS
The means must. Justify the end.
— *M. Gandhi*

MEDICINE
Like cures like.
— *Hahenmon*

God heals and the doctor takes the fee.
— *Franklin*

Better to hunt in fields for health unbought.
Than fee the doctor for a nauseous draught.
— *Dryden*

MEDIOCRITY
Thou priceless jewel, only mean men have. But cannot value.
— *Fletcher, Queen of Corinth*

MEEK
Blessed are the meek; for they shall inherit the earth.
— *New Testament, Mathew*

MEEKNESS
The flower of meekness grows on stream of grace.
— J. Montgomery

MEETING
Journey end in lover's meeting,
Every wise man's son doth know.
— Shakespeare, Twelfth Night

In life there are meetings which seem like a fate.
— Owen Meredith

MELANCHOLY
I am not merry, but I do beguile.
The thing I am, by seeming otherwise.
— Shakespeare, Othello

If there be a hell upon earth, it is to be found in melancholy—man's heart.
— Burton

MEMORY
You leave your memory as a flame to my lovely lamp of separation.
— Tagore

This is the truth the poet sings
That sorrow's crown is remembering happier things.
— Tennyson, Locksely Hall

The memory strengthens as you lay burdens upon it.
—D. Quincey

Vanity play lurid tricks with our memory
— Joseph Canrad

MERCY
We do pray for mercy and that same prayer doth teach us all to render the deeds of mercy.
— Shakespeare, Merchant of Venice

Blessed are the merciful : for they shall obtain mercy.
— New Testament, Mathew

MERIT
Honour and shame from no condition rise;
At well your part; there all the honour lies.
— Pope, Essays on Man

Charms strike the sight but merit wings the sout.
— *Pope*

MERRIMENT
A merry heart maketh a cheerful countenance.
— *Old Testament*

METAPHYSICS
Metaphysics is the anatomy of the soul.
— *De Bouffless*

METHOD
The shortest way to do many things is to do only one thing at a time.
— *Cecil*

MIDNIGHT
Midnight-that hour of night's black arch the keystone.
— *Burns*

The dreadful dead of dark midnight.
— *Shakespeare*

Once upon a midnight dreary, while I pondered weak and weary.
— *Roe*

MIGHT
I proclaim that might is right, justice the interest of the stronger.
— *Plato, The Public*

Let us have faith that right makes might, and in that faith let us to the end dare to do our duty as we understand it.
— *A. Lincoln, Address, 1860.*

MIND
The mind is the man.
— *Bacon, In Praise of Knowledge*

God is mind, and God is infinite, hence all is mind.
— *Mary Baker Eddy*

A feeble body weakens the mind.
— *Rousseau*

MINORITIES
Vote should be weighed, not counted.
— *Schiller*

MIRACLES
The one miracle which God works ever more is Nature, and imparting himself to the mind.
— *Emerson*

MIRTH
Mirth makes the banquet sweet.
— *Chapman, Blind Beggar*

Nothing is so hopeless than a scheme of merriment.
— *Johnson*

MISCHIEF
But when to mischief mortal bend their will,
How soon they find fit instruments of ill !
— *Pope, The Rape of the Lock*

Now let it work; mischief thou art afoot;
Take thou what course thou wilt.
— *Shakespeare, Julius Caesar*

MISERY
If misery loves company, misery has company enough.
— *Thoreau*

Meagre were his looks,
Sharp misery had worn him to the bones.
— *Shakespeare, Romeo and Juliet*

Misry acquaints a man with strange bed fellows.
— *Shakespeare*

MISFORTUNE
When sorrows come, they come not single spies,
But in battalions.
— *Shakespeare, Hamlet*

I am a man.
More sinned against than sinning.
— *Shakespeare, King Lear*

MISTRESS
Chaste to her husband, frank to all beside,
A teeming mistress, but barren bride.
— *Pope, Moral Essays*

MOB
The fickle mob.
— *Claudian*

MODERATION
To climb steep hills requires slow pace at first.
— *Shakespeare*

Over thy doors of every school of Art I would have this one word, relieved out in deep letter of pure gold.
— *Ruskin, Modern Painters*

MODESTY
It is easy but it is a fine thing nevertheless to be Modest when one is great.
— *Voltaire*

A modest man never talks himself.
— *La Bruyere*

MONARCHY
No worthier victim and none more acceptable can be sacrificed to jove than an evil minded King.
— *Seneca*

MONEY
Put not your trust in money, but put your money in trust.
— *O.W. Holmes*

Ready money is Alladin's lamp.
— *Byron*

I cannot afford to waste my time making money.
— *Agassiz*

Gold is the touchstone whereby to try men.
— *Fuller, The Good Judge*

For the love of money is the root of all evil.
— *New Testament*

Who steals my purse steals trash.
— *Shakespeare*

MONUMENTS
I would much rather have men ask why I have no statue than why I have one.
— *Marcus Cato*

Death comes ever to monumental stones, and names inscribed thereon.

— *Ausonius*

Those only deserve a monument who do not need one.

— *Hazlitt*

MOON

The orbed miden, with white fire landen.
Whom mortals call the moon.

— *Shelley, The Cloud*

The moon was a ghostly galleon tossed upon cloudy seas.

— *Alfred Noyes*

Late, late yestreen I saw the new moon.
Wi' the auld moon in the arm.

— *Anon, Sir Patrick Spencer*

MORALITY

Morality knows nothing of geographical boundaries or distinction of race.

— *H. Spencer*

Love would turn to poison unless it is strictly limited by moral considerations.

— *M. Gandhi*

MORNING

Full many a glorious morning have I seen
Flatter the mountain-tops with sovereign eye.

— *Shakespeare*

MORTALITY

All flesh is grass, and all goodliness thereof is as the flower of the fields.

— *Old Testament*

All men think all mortal but themselves.

— *Young*

MOTHER

Her children arise and call her blessed.

— *Old Testament, Proverbs*

What is a home without a mother.

— *Alice Hawthorne*

MOTIVES

A man must be judged by his action, not the motive prompting it. God alone knows men's hearts.

— *M. Gandhi, Delhi Diary*

MOURNING

It is better to go to the house of mourning than to go to the house of feasting.

— *Old Testament, Ecclesiastes*

I count it crime.
To mourn for any over much.

— *Tennyson, in Memoriam*

MOUTH

Mouth, In man the gateway to the soul; in woman, the outlet of heart.

— *Bierce*

MURDER

Ye each man kills the thing he loves.

— *Oscar Wilde*

For murder, though it has no tongue, will speak.
With most miraculous organ.

— *Shakespeare, Hamlet*

MUSE

Alas ! what boots it with incessant care.
To tend the homely, slighted shepherd's trade,
And strictly mediate the thankless Muse ?

— *Milton, Lycidas*

MUSIC

Music is the speech of angels.

— *Carlyle*

The world speaks to me in pictures, my soul answers in music.

— *Tagore, Fireflies*

In notes, with many a winding bout
Of linked sweetness, Long drawn out.

— *Milton, L'Allegro*

Music is the medicine of breaking heart.

— *A. Hunt*

Music, when soft voices die.
Vibrates in memory.

— *Shelley*

MYSTERY

Mystery magnifies danger as the fog the sun.

— *C.C. Colton, Lacon*

Mystery is the wisdom of blockheads.

— *Horace Walpole*

MYTHOLOGY

Mythology is the religious sentiment growing wild.

— *Schilling*

N

NAME
Giving a name, indeed is a poetic art : All poetry, if we go to that with it, is but a giving of names.
— *Carlyle*

NATIONS
You can judge off the growth of a nation by finding out which class of that nation, in a particular period of history, is held in honour and repute more than the others.
— *Jawaharlal Nehru*

Nations, like individuals, are made, not only by what they acquire, but by what they resign.
— *S. Radhakrishnan*

NATURE
Nature does not proceed by leaps.
— *Linnaeus, Philosphia Eotanica*

Nature is not governed, except by obeying her.
— *Bacon, Aphorism*

Study nature as the countenance of God.
— *Charles Kingsley*

Nature never did betray the heart that loved her.
— *Wordsworth, Tintern Abbey*

NECESSITY
Necessity is the mother of invention.
— *Anon*

There is no necessity to live in necessity.
— *Seneca*

There is no virtue like necessity.

— *Shakespeare*

NEGLECT

Self-love is not so vile a sin as self neglecting.

— *Shakespeare*

NEGRO

Can the Ethiopian change his skin, or the leopard his spots ?

— *Old Testament, Jerem*

NEIGHBOUR

In the field of world policy I would dedicate this nation to the policy of the good neighbour.

— *Franklin*

When your neighbour's house is on fire, your own property is at stake.

— *Horace*

NEUTRALITY

A wise neutral joins with neither, but uses both as his honest interest leads him.

— *William Penn*

NEWS

For evil news rides post, while good news baits.

— *Milton, Samson Agonistes*

News are as welcome as the morning air.

— *Chapman*

NEWSPAPERS

Newspapers always excite curiosity. No one ever lays one down without a feeling of disappointment.

— *Lamb, Thoughts on Books*

Newspapers are the world's mirrors.

— *Jame Ellis*

In these days we fight for our ideas; and newspapers are our fortresses.

— *Heine*

NEWTON
Nature and nature's laws lay hid in Night;
God said, Let Newton be ! and all was Light.
— *Pope*

NICKNAME
A nickname is the heaviest stone the devil can throw at man.
— *Anonymous*

NIGHT
Come, civil night.
Thou sober-suited matron, all in black...
With the black mantel.
— *Shakespeare, Romeo and Juliet*

The prelude of the night is commenced in the music of the sunset, in its solemn hymn to the ineffable dark.
— *Tagore, Stray Birds*

NIGHTINGALE
O, nightingale, that on you bloomy spray,
Warblest at eve, when all the woods are still.
— *Milton*

NOBILITY
The nobel in every thought and every deed.
— *Longfellow*

How'ever it be, it seems to me,
'Tis only nobel to be good.
—*Tennyson, Lady Clare Vere be Vere*

NONSENSE
For daring nonsense seldom fails to hit.
Like scattered short, and pass with some for wit.
— *S. Butler, Modern Critics*

A little nonsense now and then;
Is relished by the best of men.
— *Anon*

NOSE
Cleopatra's nose; had it been shorter, the whole aspect of the world would have been altered.
— *Pascal, Penseas*

NOVEL
   Novels do not force their readers to sin; but only instruct them.
   — *Rimmermaun*

NOVELTY
   It is the nature of man to be greedy for novelty.
   — *Pliny The Elder*

   Human nature is greedy of novelty.
   — *Pliny*

   The novelty of noon is out of date by night.
   — *Robert Hillary*

   To innovate is not to reform.
   — *Burke*

NUDITY
   And they were both naked, the man and his wife and were not shamed.
   — *Old Testament, Genesis*

NUMBER
   And if you want it, he makes a reduction on taking a quantity.
   — *Sir W.S. Gilbert, Sorcerer.*

O

OATH
Let my right hand forget her cunning.— Let my tongue cleave to the roof of my mouth.
— *Old Testament, Psalms*

You depend upon it, the more oath taking, the more lying generally among the people.
— *Coleridge, Table Talk*

OBEDIENCE
Obedience is the mother of success and is wedded to safety.
— *Aeschylus*

Obedience alone gives the right to command.
— *Emerson*

Let them obey that know not how to rule.
— *Shakespeare*

OBLIGATION
An extraordinary haste to discharge an obligation is a sort of ingratitude.
— *Rochefoucauld*

OBSCURITY
Men who lived and died without name.
Are the chief heroes in the sacred list of fame.
— *Swift, To the Athenian Society.*

OBSERVATION
Some are more strongly affected by the facts of human life; others by the beauty of earth and sky.

Men are born with two eyes but with one tongue in order that they should see twice as much as they say.
— *C.C. Colton, Lacon*

Each one sees what he carries in his heart.

— *Geothe*

OBSTINACY

Where obstinacy takes his study stand.
To disconcert what Policy has planned.

— *Cowper, Expostulation*

There are few, very few, that will own themselves in a mistake.

— *Swift*

OCCUPATION

Absence of occupation is not rest.
A mind quite vacant is a mind distress'd.

— *Cowper, Retirement*

The busy have no time for tears.

— *Byron*

A man who has no office to go to — I don't care who he is— is a trial of which you can have no conception.

— *G.B. Shaw, Irrational Knot*

Occupation is the scythe of time.

—*Napolean*

Roll on; thou deep and dark-blue ocean, roll !

— *Byron, Childe Harold*

OFFICE

Five of things are requisite to a good officer—ability, clean hands, despatch, patience and impartiality.

— *Penn*

Public office is the last refuge of the incompetent.

— *Rose*

OLD AGE

Old age plants more wrinkles in the mind than in the face.

— *Montaigue*

Few envy the consideration enjoyed by the oldest inhabitants.

— *Emerson*

OMNIPOTENCE

My faith hath no bed to sleep upon but omnipotency.

— *Rutherford*

OPINION
So many men, so many minds.
— *Terence, Phormio*

Opinion of good men is but knowledge in the making.
— *Milton, Ateopagitica*

The masses procure their opinions ready made in open market.
— *Colton*

Opinion's but a fool, that makes us scan,
The outward habit by the inward man.
— *Shakespeare*

OPPORTUNITY
Man's extremity is God's opportunity.
— *John Flave*

There is a tide in the affairs of men,
Which, taken at the flood, leads on to Fortune.
— *Shakespeare, Julius Caesar*

We must beat the iron while it is hot : but we may polish it at leisure.
— *Dryden, Dedication of Aneid*

OPPOSITION
Opposition inflames the enthusiast; never converts him.
— *Schiller*

The oldest bodies warm with opposition, the hardest sparkle in collision.
— *Junius*

OPTIMISM
The place where optimism most flourishes is the lunatic asylam.
— *Havelock Ellis*

God's in His Heaven
All's right with the world !
— *R. Browning*

OPTIMIST AND PESSIMIST
The optimist proclaims that we live in the best of the possible words; and the pessimist fears this is true.
— *Branch Cabell*

ORATORY

All epoch-making revolutionary events have been produced not by the written but by the spoken word.
— *Adolf Hitler, Mein Kempf*

In oratory, the greatest art is to conceal art.
— *Swift*

ORDER

A place for everything and everything in its place.
— *Samuel Smiles, Thrift*

Have a place for everything and have everything in its place.
— *Anon*

Order is Heaven's first law; and this confest,
Some are and must be greater than the rest.
— *Pope, Essay on Man*

ORIGINALITY

Originality, I fear, is too often only undetected and frequently unconscious plagiarism.
— *W.R. Inge, Wit and Wisdom*

All good things which exist are the fruit of originality.
— *J.S. Will, Freedom*

He left off reading altogether; to the great improvement of his originality.
— *Charles Lamp*

ORNAMENT

All finery is a sign of littleness.
— *Lavaeter*

ORPHAN

He reminds me of the man who murdered both his parents and then, when sentence was about to be announced, pleaded for mercy on the grounds that he was an orphan.
— *Lincoln*

OSTENTATION

Does it come to this, that your knowledge is nothing to you unless some other person knows that you know it.
— *Persius*

OUTSPOKEN
　　His heart's his mouth;
　　What his breast forges that his tongue must vent.
　　　　　　　　　　　　　　— *Shakespeare, Coriolanus*

OX
　　As an ox goeth of the slaughter.
　　　　　　　　　　　　　　— *Old Testament, Jeremiah*

OXFORD
　　Home of lost cause, and forsaken beliefs, and unpopular names and impossible loyalties !
　　　　　　　　　　　　　　— *Mathew Arnold, Essay on Criticism*

P

PAIN
    One fire burns out another's burning;
    One pain lessen'd by another' anguish.
                      — *Shakespeare, Romeo and Juliet*
    There are two things to be sanctified : pain and pleasure.
                                   — *Pascal, Panseas*

PAINTING
    I mix them with my brains, sir.
                                            — *Joen Opie*
    A picture is a poem without words.
                                               — *Horace*
    No author can live by this work and be as empty headed as an average successful painter.
                                           — *G.B. Shaw*
    Paint me as I am. If you leave out the scars and wrinkles, I will not pay you a shilling.
                                  — *Oliver Cromwell*

PANIC
    A Panic is stampede of our self-possession.
                                               — *Rivarol*

PARADISE
    For he on honey drew hath fed.
    And drunk the milk of Paradise.
                                — *S.T. Coleridge, Kubla Khan*

PARDON
    They who forgive most, shall be most forgiven.
                                               — *Bailey*

To understand is to pardon.
— *Madame De Stael*

PARENTS
Children begin by loving their parents; as they grow older they judge them : sometimes they forgive them.
— *Oscar Wilde, The Picture of Dorian Gray*

The voice of parents is the voice of Gods, for to their children they are heaven's lieutenants.
— *Shakespeare*

PARLIAMENT
Beautiful talk is by no means the most pressing wants in Parliament.
— *Carlyle, Latter Day Pamphlets*

PARTING
I have no parting sigh to give, so take my parting smile.
— *L.E. Landor*

Good night, good night ! parting is such sweet sorrow, that I shall say good night till it be morrow.
— *Shakespeare, Romeo and Juliet*

PARTIES
Party spirit which, at best, is but the madness of many for the gala of few.
— *Pope*

PASSIONS
Conquest of passion is bound up with the conquests of the palate.
— *M. Gandhi*

It is with our passions, as it is with fire and water they are good servants but bad masters.

Where passion rules, how weak does reason prove.
— *Dryden, Rival Ladies*

PAST
Let the dead past bury its dead.
— *Longfellow, A Psalm of Life*

The best friend one can have is the past.
— *Baroness De Krudener*

Not heaven itself upon the past has power.

— *Dryden*

PATIENCE

Hope and patience will achieve more than our force.

— *Burke, Reflection on the Revolution*

Patience and perseverance overcome mountain passion.

— *La Fontaine*

Patience and perseverance overcome mountain.

— *M. Gandhi*

A patient man's pattern for a king.

— *Dekker, Honest Whore*

PATRIOTISM

Patriotism is the last refuge of a scoundrel.

— *Johnson, Remarks*

You'll never have a quiet world till you knock the patriotism out of the human race.

— *G.B. Shaw*

PATRONAGE

Maecenas, sprung from royal stock, my bulwark and my glory dearly cherished.

— *Horace, Odes*

PEACE

Peace itself is war in masquerade.

— *Dryden, Absalom and Achitoyhel*

Peace is such a precious jewel that I would give any thing for it but truth.

— *M. Henry*

Peace with honour.

— *Disraeli*

PEARL

...... neither cast ye your pearls before swine, lest they trample them under their feet.

— *New Testament, Mathew*

PEASANTRY

But a hold peasantry, their country, pride.
When once destroy'd can never be supplied.
— Goldsmith, Deserted Village

PEDANTRY

Pedantry crams our heads with learned lumber and takes out our brains to make room for it.
— Colton

PEDIGREE

To have the feeling of gentility it is necessary to have been born gentle.
— Lame

PEN

A pen becomes a clarion.
— Longfellow

PENGUIN

The penguin flies backwards because he doesn't care to see, where he's going, but wants to see where he's been.
— Faced Allen, The Backward View

PERCEPTION

The heart has eyes that the brain knows nothing of.
— C.H. Parkhurst

PERFECTION

Bachelor's wives and old maid's children are always perfect.
— Chemfort

Take away the idea of perfection, and you take away enthusiasm.
— Rousseau, Juliet

PERFUME

All the perfumes of Arabia will not sweeten this little hand.
— Shakespeare, Mathew

PERSEVERANCE

Victory belongs to the most persevering.
— Napolean

PERSISTENCE
Obstinacy in a bad cause is but canstancy in a good.
— *Sir T. Browne, Religo Medical*

PERSONALITIES
Personality is to man what perfume is to a flower.
— *Charles M. Sehwab*

When you have a good cause never descend to personalities.
— *M. Gandhi, Incidents of Gandhiji's Life*

PERSUASION
There are two levels for moving men-interest and fear.
— *Napolean*

PHILOSOPHY
Philosophy is the art of living.
— *Plutarch*

Philosophy is the highest music.
— *Plato*

Philosophy triumphs easily over ills past and ills to come; present ills triumph over philosophy.
— *La Rochefoucauld*

It is a great advantage for a system of philosophy to be substantially true.
— *Santayana*

PHYSIC
We have not only multiplied disease, but we have made them more fatal.
— *Dr. R. Rush*

PHYSIOGNOMY
Trust not too much to an enchanting face.
— *Virgil*

PITY
Soft pity enters at iron gate.
— *Shakespeare, Lucrece*

In pity for the desolate branch spring leaves to kiss it that fluttered in a lonely leaf.
— *Tagore, fireflies*

PLEASURE
Consider pleasures as they depart not as they come.
— *Aristotle*

Pleasure's sin, and sometimes sin's a pleasure.
— *Byron*

PLEDGE
We mutually pledge to each other our lives, our fortunes and our sacred honour.
— *Jefferson*

POET
A poet is a nightingale who sits in darkness and sings to cheer its own solitude with sweet sound.
— *Sheller, A Defence of Poetry*

POETRY
Not marble nor the gilded monuments,
Of princes, shall outlive this powerful rhyme.
— *Shakespeare*

Poetry is the record of the best and the happiest monnments of the happiest and best minds.
— *Shelley*

POISON
What's one man's poison, signor,
Is another's meat or drink.
— *Beaumont*

POLICY
And policy regained what arms had lost.
— *Byron, Childe Harold*

To manage men out to have a sharp mind in a velvet sheath.
— *George Eliot*

POLITENESS
To be over-polite is to be rude.
— *Proverb*

The first rule of education in all lands is never to say anything offensive to anyone.
— *Voltaire, On Satire*

POLITICS
There is no gambling like politics

— *Disraeli*

POLITICIANS
Patriots are grown too shrewd to be sincere.
And we too wise to trust them

— *Cowper, Winter Morning Walk*

An honest politician is one who, when he is bought, will stay bought.

— *Simon Cameron*

POORHOUSE
Over the hill to the poorhouse I'm trudging my weary way.

— *Will Carleton, Over the Hill to the Poorhouse*

POPULARITY
Avoid popularity; it has many shares, and no real benefit.

— *Penn*

God will not love thee less, because men love thee more.

— *M.F. Tupper, Of Tolerance*

You all did love him once, not without cause.

— *Shakespeare, Julius Caesar*

POPULATION
No country can be overpopulated, if there is work for everyone.

— *Jawaharlal Nehru*

POSITION
Better to reign in Hell than serve in heaven.

— *Milton, Paradise Lost*

The higher we rise, the more isolated we become; all elevations are cold.

— *De Bouffers*

POSITIVE
To be positive : to be mistaken at the top of one's voice.

— *Ambrose Bierce*

Everyone of his opinion appears to himself to be written with sunbeams.

— *Watts*

POSSESSION
It is not lawful for me to do what I will with mine own.
— *New Testament, Mathew*

The thing possessed is not the thing it seems.
— *S. Deniel, Civil Wars*

Possession is nine points of the law.
— *Thomas Fuller*

POSTERITY
People will not look forward to Posterity, who never look backward to their ancestors.
— *Edmund Burke*

A foreign nation is a contemporaneous posterity.
— *A.P. Stanley*

POVERTY
Poverty is not vice, but an inconvenience.
— *John Floiro*

No one should praise poverty but who is poor.
— *Sir Burnard, Sermon*

Blessed be ye poor, for yours is the kingdom of God.
— *New Testament*

POWER
Power comes from sincere service.
— *M. Gandhi, Delhi Dairy*

All human power is compound of time and patience.
— *Balzac*

PRACTICE
It has been a rule of my life never to ask any one to anything which I had not tried out of practice myself.
— *M. Gandhi, An Interpretation*

Constant practice often excels even talent.
— *Cicero*

Out of the mouths of babes and sucklings thou has perfected praise.
— *New Testament, Mathew*

PRAISE

Our praises are our wages.
— *Shakespeare, Winter's Tale*

It is not he that searches for praise finds it.
— *Rivaral*

PRAYER

They never sought in vain that sought the Lord aright !
— *Burns*

Prayer needs no speech.
— *M. Gandhi, Autobiography*

The fewer words, the better prayer.
— *Luther*

When the Gods wish to punish us they answer our prayers.
— *Oscar Wilde, An Ideal Husband*

PREACHING

He preaches well who lives well.
— *Cervantes, Don Quixote*

The world is dying of want, not of good preaching but of good hearing.
— *G.D. Broadman*

PRECEDENTS

A precedent embalms a principle
— *Disraeli*

One precedent creates another. They soon accumulate and become law.
— *Julius, Dedication*

PREFACE

Reader, now I send thee, like a bee, to gather honey out of flowers and weeds : every garden furnished with either and so is ours. Read and meditate.
— *H. Smith*

PREJUDICE

It is never too late to give up your prejudice.
— *Thoreau Walden*

Prejudice is the child of ignorance.

— *Hazlitt*

PREPAREDNESS

Speak softly and carry a big stick; you will go far.

— *Roosevelt*

PRESENT

Each present joy or sorrow seems the chief.

— *Shakespeare*

Ah, take the Cash, and let the Credit go
Nor heed the rumble of a distant Drum;

— *Omar Khayyam*

PRESS

Four hostile newspapers are more to be feared than a thousand bayonets.

— *Napoleon*

Blessed are they who never read a newspaper, for they shall see Nature and through her God.

— *Thoreau*

PRETENSION

Who makes the forest show, means most deceit.

— *Shakespeare*

PRIDE

Pride is at the bottom of all great mistakes.

— *Ruskin, Modern Painters*

Pride is increased by ignorance; those assume the most who know the least.

Pride goeth before destruction and haughty spirit before a fall.

— *Old Testament*

PRINCE

Put your trust in princes.

— *Old Testament*

PRINCIPLE

Principle a passion for truth and right.

— *Hazlitt*

PRISON
Prisons are built with stones of Law, brothers with bricks of Religion.
— *Back, Proverbs of Hell*

PRIVACY
No more privacy than a goldfish.
— *H.H. Munro*

PROCRASTINATION
Never put off till tomorrow that what you can do today.
— *Frankline*

PROFANITY
Ill deeds are doubled with an evil word.
— *Shakespeare*

PROGRESS
Progress is a lame woman. It can only come hopping.
— *M. Gandhi, Young India*

Every step of progress, the world has made, has been from scaffold to scaffold and from stake to stake.
— *Wendell Phillips*

Progress is the activity of today and assurance of tomorrow.
— *Emerson*

PROHIBITION
Our country has deliberately undertaken a great social and economic experiment, noble in motive and far-reaching in purpose.
— *Herbert Hoover*

PROMISE
We promise according to our hopes, and perform according to our fears.
— *La Rochefoucauld*

Promise, is a promise, is the soul of an advertisement.
— *Johnson, Idler*

PROPERTY
The magic of property turns sand to gold.
— *Jeremy Benthan*

Property has its duties as well as its rights.
— *T. Drummond*

PROPHECY
Your sons and your daughters shall prophecy, your old men shall dream dreams, young men shall see visions.
— *Old Testament*

PROPHETS
Beware of false prophets, which come to you in sheep's clothing, but inwardly they are ravening wolves.
— *New Testament*

You can scarcely answer a prophet : you can only disbelieve him.
— *Cowper, Of Pitt's Prediction*

PROSPERITY
Greater virtues are necessary in bearing good fortune than bad.
— *La Rochefoucaul*

In prosperity prepare for a change : in adversity hope for one.
— *Burgh*

PROVERBS
Proverbs are short sentences, drawn from long experience.
— *Cervantes, Don Quixote*

PROVIDENCE
Are not two sparrows sold for farthing ? and one of them shall not fall on the ground without your Father.
— *New Testament, Mathew*

We must follow, not force Providence.
— *Shakespeare*

PRUDENCE
Festination may prove precipitation; Deliberating delay may be wise cunctation.
— *Browne*

PUBLIC
The public be damned
— *W.H. Vanderbilt*

Better be three hours soon than one minute late.

— *Shakespeare*

PUNISHMENT

Men are not hanged for stealing horses, but that horses may not be stolen.

— *Lord Helifax*

Anger to be very specially avoided inflicting punishment.

— *Cicero*

Punishment is lame, but it comes.

— *Herbert*

PURITY

Blessed are the pure in heart; For they shall see God.

— *New Testament, Mathew*

QUARRELS

Quarrels will not last long if the wrong were only on one side.
— *La Rochefoucauld*

In a false quarrel there is true valour.
— *Shakespeare*

QUESTION

What songs the Sirens sang or what name Achilles assumed when he hid himself among the women though puzzling questions are not beyond all conjecture.
— *Sir Thomas Browne*

QUIET

Sometimes quiet is disquieting.
— *Seneca*

What sweet delight a quiet life affords.
— *Drummond*

QUOTATION

Some for renown, on scraps of learning dote,
And think they grow immortal as they quote.
— *Edward Young, Love of Fame*

Next to the originator of a good sentence is the first quoter of it. Many will read the book before one things of quoting a passage.
— *Emerson, Quotations and Originality*

R

RAGE

In rage deaf as the sea; hasty as fire.

— *Shakespeare*

RAILWAY

Your railroad, when you come to understand it, so only a device for making the world smaller.

— *Ruskin, Modern Painters*

RAIN

He sendeth rain on the just and the unjust.

— *New Testament, Mathew*

The sunshine greets me with a smile. The rain, his sad sister, talks to my heart.

—*Tagore, Stray Birds*

The kind refresher of the summer heart.

— *Thomson*

RAINBOW

I do set my bow in the clouds, and it shall be for a token of a covenant between me and the earth.

— *Old Testament, Genesis*

That smiling daughter of the storm.

— *Colton*

RANK

Through tattered clothe, small vices do appear Robes and furred gowns hide all.

— *Shakespeare, Lear*

Rank and riches are chains of gold, but still chains.

— *Runffine*

RASHNESS
For fools rush in where angels fear to tread.
— *Pope, Criticism*
Rashness and haste make all things insecure.
— *Benham*

READING
It is well to read everything of something and something of everything.
— *Brougham*
Reading is to the mind, what exercise is to the body.
— *Steele*
The art of reading is to skip judiciously.
— *P.G. Hamerton*

REASON
The heart has reasons of which reason has no knowledge.
— *Pascal*
Good reason must, of force, give place to better.
— *Shakespeare*

REBELLION
Rebellion against tyranny is obedience to God.
— *Franklin*
Rebellion to tyrants is obedience to God.
— *Anon*

RECOMPENSE
Mercy to him that shows it, is the rule.
— *Cowper*
Recreation is not the highest kind of enjoyment, but in its time and place is quite as proper as prayer.
— *S.I. Prime*

REDEEMER
I know that my redeemer liveth.
— *Old Testament*

REFINEMENT
To great refinement is false delicacy, and true delicacy is solid refinement.
— *Rochefoucauld*

REFLECTION
He that will not reflect is a ruined man.
— *Proverb*

REFORM
Every reform movement has a lunatic fringe.
— *Theodore Roosevelt*

To reform a man you must begin with his grandfather.
— *Victor Hugo*

REGRET
I only regret that I have but one life to lose for my country.
— *Nathan Hale*

RELATIVES
God gives us relatives; thank God we can choose our friends.
— *Addison Misner*

RELIEF
For this relief much thanks : 'tis bitter cold,
And I am sick at heart.
— *Shakespeare, Hamlet*

RELIGION
We have just enough religion to make us hate, but not enough to make us love one another.
— *Swift*

Religion is the conquest of fear; the antidote to failure and death.
— *S. Radhakrishnan*

There is only one religion, though there are a hundred versions of it.
— *G.B. Shaw*

REMEMBRANCE
Sweet is the remembrance of troubles when you are in safety.
— *Euripides*

Praising what is lost makes the remembrance dear.
— *Shakespeare*

REMORSE
Consider it not so deeply.
— *Shakespeare, Macbeth*

Farewell, remorse : all good to me is lost :
Evil, be thou my good.

— *Milton, Paradise Lost*

Remorse is the echo of a lost virtue.

— *Bulwer*

REPENTANCE

Joy shall be in heaven over one sinner that repenth, more than over ninety and nine just persons which need no experience.

— *New Testament, Luke*

Try what repentance can : What can it not ?
Yet what can it, when one cannot repent ?

— *Shakespeare, Hamlet*

Hearty, repentance broke the edge of guilt and led the way to proper understanding.

— *M. Gandhi, Delhi Diary*

Before God can deliver us we must undeceive ourselves.

— *Augustine*

REPOSE

The best of men have ever loved repose.

— *Thompson*

Our foster-nurse of nature is repose.

— *Shakespeare*

Repose is a special separating characteristic of the eternal mind and power.

— *Ruskin, Modern Painters*

REPUBLIC

Republic end through luxury; monarchies through poverty.

— *Montesquiev, Spirit of Law*

REPUTATION

Good name in man or woman, dear my lord, is the immediate jewel of their souls.

— *Shakespeare, Othello*

Seeking the babble reputation
Even in the cannon's mouth.

— *Shakespeare*

RESIGNATION

It's no use crying over spilt milk; it only makes it salty for the cat.

Submission to God is the only balm that can heal the wound He gives.

— *Emmons*

RESOLUTION

Experience teacheth that resolution is a sole help in need.

And this the native hue of resolution.
Is sicklled o'er with pale cast of thought.

— *Shakespeare*

RESPECTABILITY

The more things a man is ashamed of, the more respectable he is.

— *Bernard Shaw, Main and Superman*

RESPONSIBILITY

The plea of ignorance will never take away our responsibilities.

— *Ruskin, Lecture*

Responsibility walks hand in hand with capacity and power.

— *J.G. Holland*

REST

Rest, rest, perturbed spirit.

— *Shakespeare*

Come unto me, all ye that labour and are heavy laden and I will give you rest.

— *New Testament*

RESURRECTION

Earth to earth, ashes to ashes, dust to dust, is sure and certain hope of the resurrection.

— *Book of Common Prayer*

RETRIBUTION

He that diggeth a pit shall fall into it.

— *Old Testament*

God is a sure paymaster. He may not pay at the end of every week, or month, or year, but remember, He pays in the end.

— *Anne of Austria*

They have sown the wind, and they shall reap whirlwind.
— *Old Testament*

The gods are just, and of our pleasant vices.
Make instruments to plague us.
— *Shakespeare, King Lear*

REVENGE
Revenge is a kind of wild justice : which the more man's nature runs to the more ought low to weed it out.
— *Francis Bacon, Essays of Revenge*

REVOLUTION
Hope ushers a Revolution—as earthquakes are preceded by bright weather.
— *Carlyle, French Revolution*

Revolutions were always rapid.
— *Voltaire, Irene*

REWARDS
My work is rewarded in daily wages, I wait for my final value in love.
— *Tagore, Fireflies*

RICHES
A man is rich in proportion to the number of things he can afford to let alone.
— *Thoreau, Where I Lived*

Wealth is not his that has it, but his that enjoys.
— *Franklin*

Lay not heep for yourself treasure upon earth; where the rust and moth doth corrupt.
— *Books of Common Prayer*

RICH MAN
The man who dies rich dies disgraced.
— *Andrew Carnegie*

RIDDLE
What animal goes on four legs in the morning, two at noon, and three in the evening.
— *The Riddle in the Sphinx*

RIGHT
Be sure you are right. Then go ahead.
— David Crockett

I see the right and I approve it too.
— Ovid

RIGHTEOUS
Be not righteous over-much, neither make thyself overwise.
Old Testament, Ecclesiastes

RISING
Up rose the sun, and up rose Emelye.
— Chaucer, The Knight's Tale

RIVALRY
Two stars keep not their motions in one sphere.
— Shakespeare

ROAD
Any road leads to the end of the world.
— Edward Fitzgerald

ROMANCE
The worst of having romance is that it leaves you so unromantic.
— Oscar Wilde

Romance is the poetry of literature.
— Madame Neckers

Tradition wears a snowy beard, romance is always young.
— Whittier, Many Carvin

ROME
Rome was not built in a day.
— Cervantes, Don Quixote

All roads lead to Rome.
— La Fontaine

ROSE
It never will rain roses : when we want.
To have more roses we must plant more trees.
— George Eliot, The Spanish Gypsy

A Rose is a rose, is a rose, is a rose.
— Gertrude Stein

RUIN
>With ruin upon ruin, rout on rout,
>Confusion worse confounded.
>
>— *Milton, Paradise Lost*

RULERS
>The ruling passion is the passion for ruling.
>
>— *Tacitus*

RUMOURS
>Stuffing the ears of men with false report.
>
>— *Shakespeare*
>
>I believe there is nothing among mankind swifter than rumour.
>
>— *Plautus, Fragn*

RUST
>It is better to wear out than to rust out.
>
>— *Richard Cumberland*

RUTH
>Whither thou goest, I go; and where thou lodgest, I will lodge : the people shall by my people and try God my God.
>
>— *Old Testament*

S

SABBATH
The Sabbath was made for man, and not man for the Sabbath.
— *New Testament*

Sunday is the golden clasp the binds together the volume of the week.
— *Longfellow*

SACRIFICE
Woman is the embodiment of sacrifice, and therefore not violence.
— *M. Gandhi*

A life of sacrifice is the pinnacle of art and is full of true joy.
— *M. Gandhi*

SADNESS
Take my word for it, the saddest thing under the sky is a soul incapable of sadness.
— *Countess De Gasparin*

SAILORS
The wonder is always new that any sane man can be a sailor.
— *Emerson, English Traits*

SAFETY
......out of the nette, danger, we pluck this flower safety.

SAINT
There are many (questionless) canonised on earth that shall never be Saints in Heaven.
— *Sir T. Browne*

The only difference between the saint and the sinner is that every saint has a past and every sinner has a future.
— *Oscar Wilde*

A saint is a man of convictions who has been dead a hundred years, canonized now but canonaded while living.
— *H.L. Wayland*

SALE
......a man must eat a peck of salt with his friend before he knows him.
— *Cervantes, Don Quixote*

SATIETY
With pleasure drugged, he almost longed for woe.
— *Byron.*

SATIRE
Satire is a sort of glass wherein beholders do generally discover every face but their own.
— *Swift, Battle of Books*

SCANDAL
How awful to reflect that people say of us true is true.
— *L.P. Smith*

Praise undeserved is scandal in disguise.
— *Pope*

In scandal, as in robbery, the receiver is always thought as bad as the thief.
— *Lord Chesterfield*

SCENT
A woman smells of nothing.
— *Plautu*

SCEPTICISM
Scepticism is slow suicide.
— *Emerson*

SCHOLARSHIP
The world's great men have not commonly great scholars, nor its great scholars, great men.
— *O.W. Holmes, Autocrat*

SCIENCE
Science moves but slowly creeping on from point to point.
— *Tennyson, Locksley Hall*

Science is costly, more stimulating to the imagination than are the classics.

— *J.B. Haldane*

SCORN

Nor siteth in the scornful.

— *Old Testament*

SCULPTURE

Sculptures are far close akin to poetry than paintings are.

— *Kamble, Lectures on Poetry*

SEA

Praise the sea, hut keep on land.

— *Herbert*

Water, water everywhere
Not a drop to drink.

— *Coleridge, Ancient Mariner*

SECRECY

I detest secrecy as a sin.

— *M. Gandhi, Young India*

He who trusts his secrets to servant makes him master.

— *Dryden*

None are so found to secrets as those who do not mean to keep them.

— *C.C. Colton*

SEEK

Seek and ye shall find; knock and it shall be opened unto you.

— *New Testament, Mathew.*

SELF

Between the share of Me and thee there is the loud ocean, my own surging self, which I long cross.

—*Tagore, Fireflies*

SELF-CONTROL

Most powerful is he who has himself in his own power.

— *Seneca*

SELFISHNESS
Self-interest sets in motion all sorts of virtues and vices.
— *La Rochefoucauld*

SELF-KNOWLEDGE
Learn God, and thou shalt know thyself.
— *Tupper*

SELF-LOVE
He that falls in love with himself, will have no rivals.
— *Frankline*

SELF-PRESERVATION
Self-preservation is the first law of nature.
— *S. Butler*

SELF-RELIANCE
The basis of good manners is self-reliance.
— *Emerson, Behaviour*

SELF-RESPECT
Who will adhere to him that abandons himself ?
— *Sir P. Sidney*

SELF-SACRIFICE
Self-sacrifice enables us to sacrifice other people without blushing.
— *Bernard Shaw*

SELF-WILL
Lawless are they that make their wills their law.
— *Shakespeare*

SENSE
Of plain, sound sense, life's current coin is made.

SENSUALITY
Mind is at the root of sensuality.
— *M Gandhi, Self-Restraint vs. Self-Indulgence*

SERVICE
There never was a bad man that had ability for good service.
— *Bruke, Impeachment of Hastings*

He who serves the poor is great in the eyes of God.

— *M. Gandhi*

SHADOW

Some there be that shadows kiss;
Such have but a shadow's bliss;
We are but a dust and shadow.

— *Horace, Odes*

And what can be the use of him is more than I can see.

— *R.L. Stevenson, My Shadow*

SHAME

I never wonder to see men wicked, but I often wonder not to see them ashamed.

— *Swift, Thoughts on Various Subjects*

Such an act, that blurs the grace and blush of modesty.

— *Shakespeare, Hamlet*

SILENCE

Silence helps one to suppress one's anger, as perhaps nothing else does.

— *M. Gandhi*

The unspoken word never does harm.

— *Kossuth*

The rest is silence.

— *Shakespeare*

SIMPLICITY

Nothing is more simple than greatness; indeed to be simple is to be great.

— *Emerson*

Without an intelligent return to simplicity, there is no escape from our descent to a state lower than brutality.

— *M. Gandhi, Young India*

SIN

Sin is essentially departure from God.

— *Luther*

How immense appear to us the sins that we have not committed.

— *Madam Necker*

SINCERITY
A little sincerity is a dangerous thing and a great deal of it is absolutely fatal.
— *Oscar Wilde*

The sincere alone can recognise sincerity.
— *Carlyle, Heroes*

SINNER
God be merciful to me, a sinner.
— *New Testament*

SKIN
Can the Ethiopian change his skin, or the leopard his spots?
— *Old Testament*

SLAVERY
If slavery is not wrong, nothing is wrong.
— *Lincoln*

A house divided against itself cannot stand. I believe this government cannot endure permanently half-slave and half-free.
— *Lincoln*

Corrupted freemen are the worst of slaves.
— *Garrice*

SLEEP
Blessings on him that first invented sleep!
— *Cervantes, Don Quixote*

O sleep, thou ape of death, lie dull upon her!
And be her sense but as a monument.
— *Shakespeare*

How wonderful is death.
Death and his brother sleep.
— *Shelley, Queen Mab*

SMILE
One may smile, and smile, and be villain.
— *Shakespeare, Hamlet*

Eternal smiles his emptiness betray.
As shallow streams run dimpling all the way.
— *Pope*

SOCIETY
Society is no comfort to one not sociable.
— Shakespeare

SOLDIERS
When captains courageous : whom death could not daunt.
Did March to the siege of the city Gaunt.
— Anon

SOLITUDE
Alone, alone, all, all alone;
Alone all on a wide, wide sea !
— S.T. Coleridge

Solitude sometimes is best society.
— Milton, Paradise Lost

SONG
Our sweetest songs are those which tell of saddest thought.
— Shelley, Skylark

Songs have immunity from death.
— Ovid

What will a child learn sooner than a song.
— Prior, Better Answer

SOPHISTRY
Some men weave their sophistry till their own reason is entangled.
— Johnson

SORROW
Past sorrows let us moderately lament them :
For those to come, seek wisely to prevent them.
— Webester, Duchess of Molfi

When sorrows come they come not single spies, but in battalions.
— Shakespeare, Hamlet

Earth has no sorrow that heaven cannot heal.
— Thomas Moore

SOUL
Real beauty is the beauty of soul.
— M. Gandhi, Gandhiji's Life and Work

Life is the soul's nursery...it's training place for the destinies of eternity.
— *Thackeray*

The force of arms is powerless when matched against the force of love or the soul.
— *M. Gandhi, Hind Swaraj*

SPEECH
The true use of speech is not so much to express our wants as to conceal them.
— *Goldsmith, The Bee*

Out of the abundance of the heart the mouth speaketh.
— *New Testament, Mathew*

Speak the speech, I pray you, as I pronounce it to you, trippingly on the tongue.
— *Shakespeare, Hamlet*

SPIRIT
Spirit are not finely touch'd but to fine issues.
— *Shakespeare, Measure for Measure.*

SPOILS
They see nothing wrong in the rule, to the victor belong the spoils of the enemy.
— *W. M. Marcy*

SPRING
Spring unlocks the flowers to paint the laughing soil.
— *Heber*

STAGE
All the world's a stage.
And all the men and women merely players.
— *Shakespeare, As You Like It*

STARS
Two things fill the mind with ever new and increasing wonder and awe ... the starry heavens above me and the moral law within me.
— *Kant*

Ye stars, that are poetry of heaven.
— *Byron*

The stars in their courses fought against Sisera.
— *Old Testament, Judges*

STATE
I am the State !
— *Louis*

STATESMAN
A statesman's heart should always be in his head.
— *Napoleon*

STATISTICS
There are three kinds of lies, lies damned lies and statistics.
— *Disraeli*

STORMS
Blow winds and crack your cheeks ! rage ! blow !
You contracts and hurricanes, spout.
Till you have drench'd our steeples.
— *Shakespeare, King Lear*

STORY
No story is the same to us after the lapse of time; or rather we who read it are no longer the same interpreters.
— *George Eliot*

STRENGTH
'O' it is excellent
To have giants's strength : but it is tyrannous to use it like a giant.
— *Shakespeare, Measure for Measure*

STRIFE
To strive with an equal is a doubtful thing, with a superior, a mad thing, with an inferior, a vulgar thing.
— *Seneca*

STUDY
Study serves for delight, for ornament, and for ability.
— *Francis Bacon*

STYLE
Proper words in proper places.
— *Swift*

SUBLIMITY
    Sublimity is Hebrew by birth.
                                          — Coleridge

SUCCESS
    Nothing can seem foul to those that win.
                                          — Shakespeare

SUICIDE
    Self-destruction is the effect of cowardice in the highest extreme.
                                          — Defoe

SUPERIORITY
    Never seem wiser on more learned than your company.
                                          — Lord Chesterfield

SYMPATHY
    A fellow-feeling makes us wonderous kind.
                                          — Garrick

T

TACT

Tact comes as much from goodness of heart as from fineness of taste.

— *Endymion*

TALENT

It always seems to me a sort of clever stupidity only to have one sort of talent like carrier-pigeon.

— *George Eliot*

TALK

To talk without effort is, after all the great charm of talking.

— *J.C. Hare*

TASTE

A person's taste is as much his own peculiar concern as his opinion or his own purse.

— *J.S. Mill*

Bad taste is a species of bad morals.

— *Bavee*

TAX

Taxes are the sinews of the state.

— *Cicero*

Teaching
To know how to suggest is the art of teaching.

— *Amiel*

TEMPERANCE

Abstinence is as easy to me as temperance would be difficult.

— *Johnson*

TEMPTATION
More potent than the spoken words in a pure thought.
— M. Gandhi, Harijan

It is one thing to be tempted, another thing to fall.
— Shakespeare

THOUGHT
Thinking is the talking of the soul with itself.
— Plato

TIME
Time conquers all, and we must time obey.
— Pope

I waste time and now doth time wastes me.
— Shakespeare

TOLERATION
Error tolerates, truth condemns.
— Caballero

TRAVEL
If you want to see how selfish people are, and how skindeep fashionable politeness is, take a voyage.
— G.B. Shaw-Irrational Knot

TREACHERY
It is time to fear when tyrants seem to kiss.
— Shakespeare

TREASON
Treason pleases, but not the traitor.
— Cervantes

TRIAL
There are no crown-bearers in heaven that were not cross-bearers here below.
— Spurgeon

TROUBLE
Troubles are often the tools by which God fashions us for better things.
— H.W. Beecher

TRUST
He was a gentleman on who I built an absolute trust.
— *Shakespeare, Macbeth*

TRUTH
Truth is the law of our being.
— *M. Gandhi, Gandhiji's Ideas*

While you live, tell truth and shame the devil.
— *Shakespeare*

TYRANNY
Tyranny sways, not as it hath power, but as it is suffered.
— *Shakespeare*

U

UNHAPPINESS
It is better not to be than to be unhappy.
— *Dryden*

UNKINDNESS
She hath tied sharp toothed unkindness, a vulture here.

UTILITY
Man having enslaved the elements remains himself slave.
— *Shelley, Defence of Poetry*

V

VALOUR
    The better part of volur is discretion.
                                                                 — *Shakespeare*

VANITY
    Nothing is so credulous as vanity, or so ignorant of what become itself.
                                                                   — *Shakespeare*

VARIETY
    Variety is the spice of life that gives it all its flavour.
                                                                          — *Cowper*

VENGEANCE
    Vengeance has no foresight.
                                                                         — *Napolean*

VICE
    Once vice worn out makes us wiser than fifty tutors.
                                                                       — *Bulwer*

VICTORY
    In victory the hero seeks the glory, not the prey.
                                                               — *Sit P. Sidna*

VIGILANCE
    Eternal vigilance is the price of liberty
                                                                       — *Jefferson*

VIOLENCE
    Violence delights have violent ends.
                                                                 — *Shakespeare*

VIRTUE
Good company and good discourse are the very sinews of virtue.
— *Izzak Walton*

VOICE
The voice is celestial melody.
— *Longfellow*

VOW
Unheedful vows may heedfully be broken.
— *Shakespeare*

VULGARITY
Be thou familiar, but by no means vulgar.
— *Shakespeare*

W

WANT

The fewer our wants, the nearer we resemble the gods.

— *Socrates*

WAR

War ! that made the world so love to play.

— *Swift*

WEAKNESS

To be weak is miserable, doing or suffering.

— *Milton*

WEALTH

Less coins, less care; to know how to dispense with wealth to possess it.

— *Reynold*

WELCOME

A tableful of welcome make scares one dainty dish.

— *Shakespeare*

WILL

People do not lack strength; they lack will.

— *Victor Hugo*

WIND

Ill blows the wind that profits nobody.

— *Shakespeare*

WINE

Wine invents nothing it only tattles. It lets out secrets.

— *Schillet*

WISH
   Wishing—the constant hectic of the fool.
                                                — *Young*

WIT
   Wit is the salt of conversation, not the fool.
                                                — *Hazelitt*

WOMAN
   Woman reduces all to common denominator.
                                                — *G.B. Shaw*

WORD
   The knowledge of words is the gate of scholarship.
                                                — *Milton*

WORK
   Give me love and work—these two only.
                                                — *William Morris*

WORLD
   Trust not the world, for it never payeth what is promiseth.
                                                — *Augustine*

YOUTH
Youth is a continual intoxication, it is the fever of reason.
— *Rochefoucauld*